WATERLOO
IN 100 OBJECTS

WATERLOO
IN 100 OBJECTS

GARETH GLOVER

FOREWORD BY ANDREW ROBERTS

To my long suffering but ever supportive wife Mary,
with love

First published 2015

The History Press
The Mill, Brimscombe Port
Stroud, Gloucestershire, GL5 2QG
www.thehistorypress.co.uk

British Library Cataloguing in Publication Data.
A catalogue record for this book is available from the British Library.

ISBN 978 0 7509 6289 6

Typesetting and origination by The History Press
Printed in Malta by Melita Press

Contents

Foreword by Andrew Roberts   7

Introduction   10

Waterloo in 100 Objects   15

Acknowledgements   313

Index   314

Foreword

IN THE AVALANCHE of books to commemorate the Battle of Waterloo, the distinguished historian Gareth Glover has somehow managed to come up with an idea which differentiates itself from all the rest. By hitting on the brilliant concept of choosing 100 images and objects that bring the period surrounding the battle, as well as the battle itself, so vividly to life, he has made a real contribution to the events surrounding the bicentenary, and is to be congratulated on doing it in a way that is informative, entertaining and scholarly.

It is important even two centuries later that Waterloo is remembered as a crucial punctuation mark in British history, because it signalled not only the final full-stop for Napoleon's ambitions to have hegemony over Western Europe for his French Empire, but also the start of Britain's own nineteenth-century greatness, especially once the Congress of Vienna, which also took place in 1815, rewarded it for its long campaigns against Napoleonic France with vital nodal points around the world. Although it is debatable whether Napoleon could have defeated the enormous Russian and Austrian forces marching on France in 1815 even if he had won at Waterloo, it is certain that at the battle the Duke of Wellington punctured forever any hopes Napoleon might have had to resuscitate French greatness.

With far too many schools all too often teaching ever more specialised areas of history today, with seemingly arbitrary periods being highlighted for study, Mr Glover is doing a public service in drawing a new generation's attention to the Battle of Waterloo in such an arresting and inspiring way.

To choose 100 objects from so wide a spectrum to illustrate what happened at Waterloo is a peculiarly effective way of making the battle come alive, even 200 years later. Gorgeous uniforms – see Colonel Marbot's of the French 7th Hussars, for instance – cannon, bayonets, the famous 'Brown Bess' musket and Baker rifle, maps, mausoleums, relics, medals, curiosities, orders written in Wellington's handwriting, photographs of key buildings, even the dentures made from teeth pulled out of corpses' mouths – these are just some of the truly fascinating objects that Mr Glover has identified and documented for us. They all have the power of making this vital moment in history stand out, especially when explained by his succinct yet informative short essays on each.

The result is that the momentous events of those four days in mid-June 1815 are brought to life again, as the objects tell their stories and are fitted into the whole picture. When we see Alexander Gordon's finely crafted magnifying glass, for example, we are drawn into the tale of Wellington's brave aide-de-camp who died of his wounds the day after the battle, and hear of the tears the otherwise highly emotionally reserved British commander-in-chief shed for Gordon and his other friends who had perished. A medallion of HMS *Bellerophon* struck in 1820, to quote another example, allows Glover to tell us of the surrender of Napoleon to Captain Maitland a month after Waterloo.

The nearly 100,000 people of all sides who were killed or wounded during Napoleon's 100-day adventure to try to recapture his throne in 1815 deserve a lasting memorial, and they are certainly being given one in these extensive bicentenary commemorations organised by the Waterloo 200 Committee, and this fine book is an excellent addition to its work. It is important to our sense of national identity that the more fragile of these fascinating and valuable objects be protected for posterity, so that they can be admired and reflected upon 100 years hence, on the tercentenary of the battle in 2115. This virtual collection, however, is the modern equivalent of Troop Sergeant Major Edward Cotton's museum in 1909, and Gareth Glover should be congratulated on the excellent work he has done in bringing it together for us.

Andrew Roberts

Introduction

I HAVE BEEN studying Waterloo, the final battle of the Great War, in great detail for some forty years. This opening statement will cause some bewilderment to many who have grown up with the appellation of the Great War firmly applied to the 1914–18 First World War. But to anyone living before 1918, the title of the Great War was applied to the Revolutionary and Napoleonic wars in which Britain fought France almost continuously for twenty-two years from 1793 to 1815.

The Battle of Waterloo, fought in Belgium on 18 June 1815, exactly 200 years ago, was completely decisive, ending Napoleon's hopes forever. Nine hours of bitter fighting set the course of Europe and indeed the entire world for a century. However, it must be understood that the battle does not stand alone: it was the culmination of a rapid campaign in Belgium but the allies still had to march to Paris to end Napoleon's reign again.

Despite such cataclysmic results, few people now know much about this short campaign. I have met many who thought that the battle occurred in London, assuming that the train station stands on the battle site; or they have assumed it was fought in France because they remember that Napoleon was defeated there, possibly basing their knowledge on the famous Abba song of that name. Few will know the generals who opposed him, although arguably Britain's greatest ever general fought here, and they will almost certainly know nothing of the men of other countries who fought and died there: the Prussians, the Dutch, Belgians, Brunswickers, Nassauers and Poles, and even a couple of Americans.

History as taught in our schools has for many decades hopped straight from the Stuarts to the Industrial and Agrarian Revolutions and then again to the First and Second World Wars. This shameful negation of the entire Georgian period is deliberate: this allows for the avoidance of any reference to the rise of the British Empire, which we are now expected to feel only shame for. But we ignore the lessons of any period of history at our peril and the empire, both good and bad, very much formed this country we now live in, and without an understanding of that, we can understand nothing of our past.

The Battle of Waterloo was both a fascinating and a terrible thing. War is never glorious or pretty and certainly never comes without great pain and loss for all sides engaged. But sometimes war is unavoidable and necessary as the lesser of evils, and it can change the course of history. Such was Waterloo.

The intention of this book is to fascinate and thus to educate about this whirlwind campaign which decided so much in a four-day period. Because of its significance, everybody sought to own a memento from the battlefield or a commemorative piece commissioned in its aftermath. This has meant that a huge mass of this material is still to be seen in museums and private collections across the globe; indeed, many families still lovingly treasure items relating to their forebears who fought in this momentous campaign. From this wealth of objects I have drawn 100 items that help tell the fascinating story in an engaging way: some macabre, others sad, a few may seem too incredible to be true, but they are, and others simply help us understand the trials of life and death for a soldier 200 years ago.

A brief understanding of the reasons why Waterloo occurred is perhaps necessary for those unacquainted

with the history. The French Revolution had seen the guillotining of King Louis XVI of France in 1793 and the monarchies of Europe turning on France to avoid the revolutionary spirit spreading and threatening their own thrones. Fortunes see-sawed until one man, Napoleon Bonaparte, took his chance to make his name and captured northern Italy and then Egypt for France. Once he had the army on his side, he duly organised a military takeover, becoming First Consul and within a few years Emperor of France. He transformed the war against the European monarchies, defeating the three great continental military powers, Austria, Prussia and Russia, in succession. At its height the French Empire reached from Oporto to Warsaw. Britain remained his

only constant foe; Britain ruled by sea, Napoleon by land. However, in 1812 he overstretched himself and his army of half a million men reached Moscow, but died almost to a man in the snows of a Russian winter. By 1814 France was overwhelmed and Paris fell; Napoleon was forced to abdicate and was exiled to the tiny Mediterranean island of Elba.

However, Napoleon continued to plot from his mini kingdom, and when he judged the time right he sailed with only one thousand men and landed in France on 1 March 1815. As his small force marched on Paris, the Royalist armies sent against him, simply switched allegiance and Napoleon was swept into Paris on a tide of adulation.

The great powers of Europe were still in congress at Vienna, deciding how to produce a balance of power in Europe after the break-up of the French Empire, when Napoleon returned, and they unanimously declared war against him, not France. Realising that he stood no chance against the combined armies of Europe, Napoleon hastily formed his army and launched a surprise attack on Belgium, aiming to destroy the armies of Britain and the Netherlands (Holland and Belgium being one kingdom) under the Duke of Wellington and a Prussian army under Field Marshal Blücher, before the Austrians, Russians and Spanish could enter the war. If he could destroy these armies and effectively knock those countries out of the war, he hoped the others might be brought to the peace table.

At Waterloo, over 180,000 men with over 40,000 horses fought on a battlefield no wider than three square miles, and by the end over 50,000 men and 20,000 horses were killed or severely maimed. Wellington, supported by the arrival of the Prussians, destroyed the French army, and Napoleon's dreams of a renewed French Empire were quashed forever. Napoleon was forced to abdicate once again and was exiled to the South Atlantic island of St Helena, where he died; Britain effectively turned its back on Europe and used its domination of the seas to further expand its empire, whilst Europe looked for a new way forward to try to avoid these seemingly interminable wars. The Age of Congress was born and at every crisis all the heads of Europe would meet to debate and attempt to find a peaceful solution. War was not avoided completely, but local wars were prevented from escalating into pan-European conflict for 100 years, until the Germans refused to attend a congress in 1914.

This is the compelling drama that was Waterloo.

Gareth Glover

100
Objects

I

King George III shilling

THIS SILVER SHILLING, minted in 1787, would have been current at the time of Waterloo. A coin such as this might have been used as an incentive for new recruits to the armed services. To take the king's shilling was to accept service in the navy or army and was a practice that dated back to the Civil War, with the shilling – a not inconsiderable sum for low-paid labourers – being offered as a payment for signing up. Whether you were a volunteer or pressed – coerced – the taking of the king's (or queen's) shilling denoted that you were in the forces.

The term is mentioned in a verse from a song of the time, 'Who'll be a Soldier?', which was sung to the tune we now know as 'Waltzing Matilda':

> The King he has ordered new troops onto
>   the continent,
> To strike a last blow at the enemy.
> And if you would be a soldier,
> All in a scarlet uniform,
> Take the King's shilling for Wellington and me.

A recruit theoretically was entitled to return the shilling at any point until he was made subject to martial law after being attested by a justice of the peace. Soon after that, a bounty was paid to the new recruit, which varied

Date of production:
1787

Location:
Private collection

considerably, but could be up to £23 17s 6d in 1812. At its highest the bounty was equivalent to over half a year's wages for the average unskilled worker.

The British army had reduced its numbers significantly with the ending of the wars in 1814 as British politicians sought to take the peace dividend and drastically reduce expenditure on the army and the navy. Many of the seasoned troops returned from southern Europe thoroughly tired of war, having fought in the harsh terrain of Portugal and Spain, for most of the previous six years. Their time served, many saw few prospects in remaining in the army, where promotion would now stagnate, and the idea of dying whilst garrisoning some godforsaken mosquito-infected island in the West or East Indies was not an attractive option. Many veterans therefore sought to leave the army on a pension of up to a shilling a day, a pittance which would need to be supplemented by paid work.

Napoleon's return to the French throne meant that the British government faced huge problems in supplying enough soldiers for the new war. Their embarrassment was saved to some extent by the very timely return of a large number of regiments which had been fighting the Americans in a conflict that was, in reality, a war over the sovereignty of Canada. Peace had been signed in January 1815 and the regiments arriving in English and Irish ports in April and May found themselves ordered directly on to Belgium.

But recruiting had to be ramped up again rapidly: regimental recruiting parties were sent out to ply young able-bodied men with beer and regale them with tales of daring exploits and the riches they could earn in prize money, to entice them to accept the king's shilling. Many who accepted the offer were rushed through basic training and stood and died or were horribly mutilated at Waterloo only a month or two after they had joined.

A number of regiments had very few experienced men when they arrived in Belgium, indeed the 14th Foot was described as being formed of 'mere boys'. But these boys stood and died at Waterloo just as bravely as any veteran.

2

The bicorn and coat of Napoleon

THE GREATCOAT AND plain cocked hat were Napoleon's habitual wear on campaign, almost always worn over the undress coat of the Chasseurs à Cheval of the Imperial Guard. The grey coat was so iconic that it gave rise to one of Napoleon's nicknames: *la redingote grise*.

Napoleon Bonaparte dominated Europe for a decade and was feared throughout the continent, but Waterloo was to destroy all his ambitions in a single day. Born in Corsica in 1769, the same year as Wellington, Napoleon became an artillery officer in the French army. When the Revolution began, he made a professional name for himself by helping the revolutionaries seize Toulon, then capturing northern Italy from the Austrians and invading Egypt in an attempt to destroy British India. On his return to France he adeptly turned his fame into political support to become one of a triumvirate of consuls in 1799, which essentially handed him the reins of power.

Date of manufacture: c. 1815

Location: Musée de l'Armée, Paris, France

Napoleon oversaw the rapid expansion of the French army and armed it with the most modern equipment. Napoleon further cemented his position by establishing himself as hereditary Emperor of France in 1804.

France needed to expand to pay for such massive forces, and monarchical Europe rapidly became

embroiled in a number of wars as it vainly sought to stem the tide of revolution which Napoleon brought with his armies. But Napoleon's tactics of rapid marches, concentration of forces and overwhelming artillery and cavalry swept the old European armies, still operating as they had in the times of Frederick the Great, aside with ease

By 1811 the French Empire stretched from Madrid to Warsaw; then Napoleon made the disastrous decision to march on Moscow. Despite capturing the city, he failed to force the Russians to the peace table and was eventually defeated by the Russian winter, losing 90 per cent of his half-million-strong army during the campaign.

Seeing an opportunity, Europe rose against France, and after a valiant effort to stem the tide, Paris was captured and Napoleon was forced to abdicate and exiled to the Mediterranean island of Elba.

Within a year, though, Napoleon recognised the moment was ripe for him, as there was great unrest caused by the policies of King Louis XVIII's government, and on 1 March 1815 he set foot on the shores of France once again, with a force of around one thousand men. Few in Europe thought that Napoleon had any chance of success, but as he led his small army across France towards Paris, thousands of soldiers of the king's army switched allegiance and joined his ranks. Soon the momentum was his, and he simply rode back into Paris, the king fleeing into Belgium. This sudden change of fortunes is perfectly encapsulated in the headlines of the French national newspaper *Le Moniteur*:

10 March:
The Corsican ogre has landed at Cape Juan.
11 March:
The tiger is in Gap. Troops are on their way and will stop him. He will end his miserable adventure as a homeless refugee in the mountains.
12 March:
The monster succeeded in proceeding to Grenoble.

13 March:

The tyrant is now in Lyon. Horror has caught the people.

18 March:

The usurper is some days' march distant from Paris.

19 March:

Bonaparte approaches in a hurry, but he will not succeed in advancing to Paris.

20 March:

Napoleon will be in Paris tomorrow.

21 March:

Emperor Napoleon is in Fontainebleau.

22 March:

Yesterday evening His Majesty celebrated his arrival in Paris. The jubilation cannot be described.

Napoleon's soldiers welcomed him back with great enthusiasm as they adored him, but it would be wrong to assume that all of France was so enraptured. Many areas remained loyal to the king, or were simply weary of war, and the constant conscription.

Despite protesting that he had a peaceful intent, Napoleon rapidly ordered a huge expansion of the army, recognising that all of Europe would turn on him, and indeed war was soon announced by all the great continental powers, not against France, but against the emperor himself.

Never being defensively minded and with the threat that a co-ordinated invasion by 150,000 men from each of the great powers of Britain, Austria, Prussia, Russia and Spain would overwhelm France, Napoleon sought to defeat them before they could join up. He was always at his best in co-ordinating the surreptitious concentration of forces, straining every sinew of the national effort to arm and supply his army and launching a surprise attack from an unexpected quarter on his enemies' forces. This occasion was no exception and his army was enthused to the point of exultation as it crossed the borders to instigate the Waterloo campaign in the early hours of 15 June 1815, rapidly marching to gain control of Charleroi and driving the Prussian advance guard back.

The ensuing campaign did not, as we know, end well for Napoleon, although it certainly started with great promise. In exile on the island of St Helena until his death in 1821, Napoleon and his supporters actively sought to publish critical reports of the actions of his marshals, blaming them for all of the failures of the campaign. Efforts were made to explain away Napoleon's poor performance, claiming illness and treachery. However, the reality was that the failure was more due to a complacency born of Napoleon's belief in his superiority over his opponents; modern analysis has shown that Napoleon was guilty of failing to brief his subordinates adequately and of underestimating his opponents.

3 Place Royale

JUST BEFORE MIDNIGHT on 15 June 1815 the bugles, drums and bagpipes of the allied army announced the reveille and the troops of the Allied Reserve Corps, stationed in and around Brussels, poured out into the streets from their billets as they made their way hurriedly to the assembly point of the army in the Place Royale and the adjoining Brussels Park.

The square was originally known as the Balienplein, which was the site of the Palace of Coudenberg and the main market square and place of executions. A serious

Date of construction: 1780

Location: Brussels, Belgium

fire in 1731 had destroyed the palace and it was not until 1780 that the replacement square was finished as an almost exact replica of the Place Royale in Reims. The square would have looked exactly as it does today, apart from the statue in the centre of Godfrey of Bouillon which was only placed there in 1848. The previous statue of Prince Charles of Lorraine had been melted down during the French Revolution and a tree of liberty raised in its place.

Once the men were formed in their battalions in and around the square, provisions for a march were issued and the men sank down onto the cobbles to await their orders; some even tried to catch some sleep as they had no idea when they would next get the chance. Revellers from the Duchess of Richmond's ball stepped gingerly

over the slumbering soldiers as they returned to their homes around the park, or they asked those who were awake for news.

At 3 a.m. orders were issued for the corps to march to Waterloo on the road to Nivelles. They trailed out of the gate to the Charleroi road and were followed by the Brunswick Corps, which had been stationed just outside the city. During the fighting the square became a vehicle depot for supplies moving up to the front and then an open-air hospital as the wounded began to arrive.

The square later gained great notoriety as the site of a large barricade which was erected at the eastern end and armed with a couple of cannon during the Belgian Revolution of 1830.

4 'Brown Bess' musket

ALMOST EVERY BRITISH and King's German Legion infantryman at Waterloo carried a 'Brown Bess' musket; it was the lynchpin of the British army and had been so for nearly a century in various versions or 'patterns'. This muzzle-loading smooth-bore land pattern musket and all its derivatives were used during the era of the expansion of the British Empire and acquired a symbolic importance at least as significant as its physical one.

The origin of the nickname 'Brown Bess' is uncertain. It is believed that this name first appeared towards the end of the eighteenth century, when the short pattern and India pattern versions were in wide use. The name 'Brown Bess' was used at the time as a term of poetic endearment, rather than a proper name; it may have been coined because of the colour of the walnut stock or the brown rust proofing applied to the barrel as, prior to this weapon, stocks were generally painted black. 'Bess' could have simply been an alliterative name, or possibly from the German *Buchse* (gun).

During the 1790s, a third pattern of the flintlock musket arrived, the India pattern, which differed from previous designs by being slightly lighter (just under 9lb) and shorter (39in). It had been developed

Date of manufacture:
c. 1815

Location:
Private collection

and adopted by the forces of the East India Company in 1795 and was accepted by the Board of Ordnance of the British army two years later. Over 3 million of these were eventually built and this was the version almost universally carried at Waterloo.

The accuracy of the Brown Bess was poor, as with most other muskets. The effective range is often quoted as 175 yards (160m), but the Brown Bess was often fired en masse at 50 yards (46m) to inflict the greatest damage upon the enemy. In fact, it is generally asserted that you would be very unlucky indeed to be struck by an aimed shot at 100 yards. Military tactics of the period stressed mass volleys and bayonet charges instead of individual marksmanship. The large soft lead ball could inflict a great deal of damage when it struck and the great length of the weapon allowed longer reach in bayonet engagements.

As with all similar smooth-bore muskets, it was theoretically possible to improve the accuracy of the weapon by reducing the windage; that is, using musket balls that fitted more tightly into the barrel. However, the black powder used at the time would quickly foul the barrel, making it more and more difficult to reload a tight fitting round after each shot and increasing the risk of the ball jamming in the barrel during loading. Therefore, as tactics at the time favoured close range battles and speed over accuracy, smaller and more loosely fitting musket balls were much more commonly used. The rate of fire ranged from 3 to 4 shots per minute with highly trained troops, to two shots per minute for inexperienced recruits.

The fame of the 'Brown Bess' was so great that Rudyard Kipling's poem 'Brown Bess' was dedicated to this famous weapon.

5

Ballgown

ON 15 JUNE, the evening before the army marched from Brussels to face Napoleon at Quatre Bras (see item 7), a ball was held, to which the great majority of the senior officers of the army and the rich of Brussels were invited. The hostess was Charlotte, Duchess of Richmond, who was in the city with her family. The ballgown depicted is of the style of 1815, being almost transparent and off the shoulder with short puffy sleeves.

Elizabeth Longford described it as 'the most famous ball in history', but it was a pure accident that this ball occurred just before the fighting, there being a string of balls organised for the season. There had already been balls held: by the Duke of Wellington on 26 May, on 4 June one was hosted by Sir Charles Stuart and on 9 June by Wellington again; the duke had another arranged for the 21st to celebrate his great victory at Vitoria in Spain two years previously.

There is still much contention about where the ball was actually held, but according to Lady Georgiana De Ros, a daughter of the Duchess of Richmond, the ball took place in a large room on the ground floor, connected to the Richmond residence on Rue des Cendres by an anteroom. The house had been rented from a coach builder who had used this annexe to keep his coaches in – perhaps as a showroom, as it already had rose trellis wallpaper on the walls. In a letter to

Date of production:
c. 1815

Location:
McCord Museum, Quebec, Canada

The Times which was published on 25 August 1888, Sir William Fraser reported that he had discovered the likely room used to house the ball. It was not part of the principal property that the Duke of Richmond rented on the Rue des Cendres, but was a coach house that backed onto the property and had an address in the next street, Rue de la Blanchisserie. The room was 120ft long and 54ft wide, and about 13ft high. Unfortunately the room no longer exists.

Wellington had received information prior to the ball, at around 6 p.m., that Napoleon had launched an attack, and orders for the army to prepare to march were promulgated. However, Wellington saw no issue with continuing the ball, probably seeing some advantage in having almost all his senior officers present if further orders were required to be communicated.

Captain George Bowles of the Coldstream Guards recalled how a further report, received around 11 p.m., during the ball caused Wellington to ask the Duke of Richmond if he had a good map. Retiring to his study to peruse the map, Wellington is reputed to have declared, 'Napoleon has humbugged me, by God; he has gained twenty-four hours' march on me. I have ordered the army to concentrate at Quatre Bras; but we shall not stop him there, and if so I must fight him there –' indicating the ridge at Waterloo. However, this story is suspect on many levels, not only because it is clear that the army was not ordered to march to Quatre Bras before 10 a.m. the following morning, but also because Wellington could have had no idea at this time that it would be necessary for him to retire to Waterloo.

The atmosphere in the room apparently changed dramatically when news circulated among the guests that the French had crossed the border and that the army was to march at dawn. Lady Jane Dalrymple-Hamilton, who sat for some time beside Wellington on a sofa, was struck by his preoccupied and anxious expression beneath the assumed gaiety. The idea that the ball continued and that officers completed their obligations to dance with the various young ladies before marching off is almost certainly a Victorian invention. Eyewitnesses talk more of hurried goodbyes, emotional partings and a distraught duchess!

The ball inspired a number of writers and artists in the nineteenth century. It was described in great detail by William Thackeray in *Vanity Fair* and by Lord Byron in *Childe Harold's Pilgrimage*. The ball also inspired artists, including Millais, who painted *The Black Brunswicker* in 1860 and Robert Hillingford, who painted *The Duchess of Richmond's Ball*.

Drawing of the room used for the ball, as it appeared in 1888.

On 15 June 1965 the British ambassador in Brussels held a ball to commemorate the 150th anniversary of the Battle of Waterloo and the Duchess of Richmond's ball, attended by 540 guests. This commemoration ball has now become an annual event, with the money raised going to support several charities.

6

Large telescope
used by the Duke of Wellington at Waterloo

THE DUKE OF Wellington commanded the allied army at Waterloo, facing Napoleon in battle for the first time. This very large telescope was apparently given to Countess Stanhope by the duke himself in October 1836 as one he had used in various battles, including Waterloo. It is intriguing to think that this was almost certainly the telescope he would have used throughout that day to seek out evidence of the arrival of the Prussian army. In a painting by Thomas Heaphy, Wellington appears holding this very telescope.

Field Marshal Arthur Wellesley, First Duke of Wellington (1769–1852), was born into the Anglo-Irish aristocracy, and was one of the leading military and political figures of the nineteenth century; he is often referred to simply as 'the Duke'. Wellesley was commissioned as an ensign in the British army in 1787. He served in Ireland as aide-de-camp to the Lord Lieutenant of Ireland and was also elected as a Member of Parliament in the Irish House of Commons. He purchased his colonelcy in 1796 and then saw limited action in Holland and then made his name by winning some decisive victories in India. However, others rather snootily referred to him as merely a 'sepoy general'; indeed, Napoleon often used the term against him.

Date of manufacture:
c. 1813

Location:
Chevening House, Kent, UK

Upon his return from the Indian campaign, Wellesley finally succeeded in marrying Kitty Pakenham in Dublin in 1806 – her family had previously rejected the match, deeming him a poor prospect. The marriage would later prove to be unsatisfactory and the two would spend years apart while Wellesley was campaigning, and he was linked constantly with many young ladies of society.

He rose to real prominence as a general during the Peninsular War, where he waged a six-year campaign with limited resources against a much larger French army and eventually led a successful Anglo/Portuguese/Spanish army to push the French out of Spain and invaded southern France. He was promoted to field marshal after his victory against the French at the Battle of Vitoria in 1813. Following Napoleon's exile in 1814, Wellesley served as the ambassador to France and was granted a dukedom, his brother choosing the name for him after the small town of Wellington in Somerset.

Wellington is famous primarily for his defensive style of warfare, which gave him several victories against numerically superior forces while minimising his own losses. He could, however, also perform well in an attack, given the opportunity. Both tactics were fully in evidence at Waterloo: he took up a carefully chosen defensive position, maintaining his army behind the crest of a ridge where they would be largely protected from losses until called forward to counter French moves, and he made an instant decision for an all-out attack at the end of the battle when he perceived the French army to be wobbling following the failure of the attack by the Imperial Guard. During the battle, he seemed to be everywhere. Wherever there was a crisis he was in the thick of it, taking refuge in a square of infantry when danger came too close.

Nicknamed the 'Peer' or 'Beau' because of his sartorial elegance, or more frequently 'our Atty' (short for

Arthur) by the common soldiers, he was never loved but was greatly admired. After the battle Wellington was frank in his appreciation of Blücher's support and admitted that it had been 'a close run thing'. He did feel affection and responsibility for those who fought with him; later that night he openly cried in the gloom of his room as the list of senior officers who had been killed and wounded was read out to him, and when his faithful horse Copenhagen died in 1836, Wellington buried him at Stratfield Saye and had a headstone erected to commemorate his service (see item 99).

Wellington was feted by all of the allied sovereigns and was made an honorary field marshal or a prince of most countries in Europe in gratitude for his great victory. He commanded the allied army which occupied northern France until 1818 and was instrumental in brokering a deal by which the allies gained financial recompense for the war and King Louis XVIII was relieved of the burden of feeding this army.

When his fighting days were over, Wellington continued a distinguished political career and was prime minister in 1828–30, overseeing the passage of the Catholic Relief Act in 1829. He was, however, seen as very much a conservative in a time of political radicalisation and was often vilified for his ardent desire to maintain the status quo. In later life he again found popularity as the country's 'elder statesman'; he continued as one of the leading figures in the House of Lords until his retirement and he remained commander-in-chief of the British Army until his death. He was granted a state funeral and was buried at St Paul's Cathedral. His London home, Apsley House, on the edge of Hyde Park, still retains the simple postal address 'No. 1 London'.

7

The Great Farm at Quatre Bras

QUATRE BRAS IS almost the forgotten battle of the Waterloo campaign. It occurred on 16 June 1815, two days before Waterloo.

Here, during the evening of 15 June and morning of the 16th, a small Netherlands force of infantry, supported by a few cannon, held the vital crossroads against the leading elements of Marshal Ney's force, which formed Napoleon's left wing. At the same time, Marshal Grouchy with the right wing, supported by Napoleon's Imperial Guard, faced Marshal Blücher's Prussian army at the Battle of Ligny only 5 miles away.

Much controversy surrounds the importance of the crossroads, but it is clear that Napoleon did not order Ney to take and hold the road junction until late in the morning, and he only began a serious attack in the early afternoon, but was severely hampered by the slow arrival of his allocated troops from the rear.

Date of construction:
Seventeenth century

Location:
Quatre Bras, Belgium

According to the allied plans previously agreed, Wellington actually intended to concentrate his forces at Nivelles, which would have left the Brussels road open, knowing that Napoleon could not advance on the city with the allied armies formed on each of his flanks.

However, during the morning of 16 June, Wellington arrived at Quatre Bras and decided to order his troops to concentrate here in an attempt to maintain his communications with Blücher. The ensuing battle, with both sides feeding in fresh troops as they arrived, was both fiercely contested and costly.

The confused battle saw allied infantry having to fight in head-high corn fields, where the numerous French cavalry constantly threatened to surprise units before they could form square, and where the low undulating plains meant that the infantry of both armies were very vulnerable to the numerous artillery deployed. A number of units were caught by the lancers and cuirassiers and decimated.

A great wood which bordered the western edge of the battlefield was fought over all day in very bloody close-quarters combat. It was eventually taken and held by the British Guards, but at a high cost, the guardsmen not being very adept at fighting in such terrain.

Wellington's force at the crossroads grew inexorably during the day as troops arrived after their long marches, but he remained inadequately supplied with cavalry, which were delayed on their march by confusion and misplaced orders.

Ney, who had enjoyed a comfortable supremacy in the early stages, was slowly outnumbered in infantry and cannon, but still enjoyed the advantage of a strong cavalry element. The Comte d'Erlon's corps had been marching to reinforce him, but was diverted in confused circumstances to join Napoleon at Ligny. These troops, however, appeared suddenly behind the French left at Ligny, causing consternation in the ranks, where it was feared that it was Wellington's force that had emerged. Napoleon sent aides to discover the identity of these troops, but they suddenly turned about and began marching away again. Marshal Ney had been made aware of the deviation of d'Erlon's corps and peremptorily ordered it to return as he was now in danger of being overwhelmed by Wellington. In the event, this corps failed to arrive on either battlefield in time to influence the outcome – a complete waste of 20,000 men, whose presence at either battle could well have been decisive.

The small hamlet of Quatre Bras formed the centre of Wellington's position and the great farmhouse stand-

Belgian corn concealing the author (who is 6ft tall) standing only 6ft into the vegetation – an illustration of what the infantry had to fight in at Quatre Bras.

ing there was used as a field hospital. The courtyard soon became a charnel house, with piles of corpses alongside heaps of amputated limbs simply thrown from the adjoining rooms, now turned into makeshift operating theatres. The occasional cannonball bounced into the courtyard and at one point a number of French cuirassiers – the remnants of a heroic although suicidal charge – trying to escape the hail of allied fire also rode into the yard. It is reported that they caused momentary alarm and confusion, but were all killed.

The battle ended at nightfall, with both sides holding pretty much the ground they had occupied in the morning and each side having lost nearly 5,000 men killed or wounded.

Much of the battlefield is relatively unchanged, although the wood has disappeared and the tiny hamlet at Quatre Bras is much changed. A number of farmsteads which were important in the battle still remain: Gemioncourt is a working farm, Pierrepont is now a luxury golf course, but the great farmhouse at Quatre Bras now stands abandoned and under constant threat of demolition – a shameful waste.

8 Légion d'Honneur

MANY A VETERAN of Napoleon's wars wore this medal, a Légion d'Honneur, on his uniform at Waterloo. It was a highly prized possession and became a popular item for souvenir hunters to collect from the dead on the battlefield.

In the French Revolution all French orders of chivalry were abolished. When he became First Consul, Napoleon wanted to create a reward to commend both civilians and soldiers, and so the Ordre National de la Légion d'Honneur was instituted on 19 May 1802, along the lines of old French orders of chivalry: the badges of

Date of manufacture:
Date of manufacture 1804–15

Location:
Private collection

the legion bear a resemblance to the old Ordre de Saint Louis, which also used a red ribbon.

The National Order of the Legion of Honour today is still the highest decoration in France and is divided into five degrees: Chevalier or Knight, Officer, Commander, Grand Officer, and Grand Cross.

The order's motto is *Honneur et Patrie* (Honour and Fatherland).

The legion was loosely organised after a Roman Legion, with legionaries, officers, commanders, regional 'cohorts' and a grand council. The order was open to men of all ranks and professions and was awarded purely on merit or bravery. It is noteworthy that all previous orders had shared a clear Christian background, whereas the legion has always been a secular institution. A new legionnaire had to be sworn into the order and received an annual sum according to his level, with the higher levels receiving generous amounts. At the time of Waterloo the payments were 5,000 francs (£8,000 in modern terms) to a grand cross, 2,000 francs (£3,200) to a commander, 1,000 francs (£1,600) to an officer, and 250 francs (£500) to a chevalier.

It is estimated that 35,000 of these medals had been awarded by the time of Waterloo. Although research is made difficult by the loss of the archives, it is known that three women who fought with the army were decorated with the order: Virginie Ghesquière, Marie-Jeanne Schelling and a nun, Sister Anne Biget.

Napoleon also dispensed fifteen golden collars of the legion among his family and his senior ministers; this award was abolished in 1815.

The Légion d'Honneur was prominent and very visible in the empire, the emperor always wore it, and the fashion of the time allowed for decorations to be worn most of the time. The King of Sweden apparently refused the order because he thought it was too common. Napoleon's own decorations were captured by the Prussians and were displayed in the Zeughaus (Armoury) in Berlin until 1945. Today, they are in Moscow.

9 Farm of d'En Haut

THE FARM OF d'En Haut stood in the village of Ligny and was witness to the terrible hand-to-hand fighting of the Battle of Ligny, fought on 16 June 1815, which proved to be the last victory of Napoleon's military career. The bitter fighting within the villages skirting the Ligny stream turned them into slaughterhouses.

Napoleon, having invaded Belgian territory and captured Charleroi on 15 June, drove his forces northwards to his initial goal of Brussels. As he advanced, the light Prussian forces in his front retired to the north-east, towards a position centred on Ligny village, where Marshal Blücher had determined to offer battle with his entire army.

Napoleon pushed his right wing, under the command of Marshal Grouchy, in pursuit of the retiring Prussians, whilst Marshal Ney commanded his left wing, which continued along the direct road to Brussels. Napoleon and his reserve stood behind them, fully prepared to come to the aid of whichever wing needed support.

By the morning of 16 June it appeared that the Prussians were preparing to make a stand, but Napoleon

Date of construction:
Sixteenth century

Location:
Ligny, Belgium

French cannonball embedded in the wall of Sombreffe Church.

was ignorant of Wellington's movements and ordered Ney to continue to probe towards Brussels and at all costs to prevent Wellington from joining Blücher.

The Prussians had brought their 1st, 2nd and 3rd Corps, but the 4th Corps was too distant and missed the battle. Blücher faced the French with 83,000 troops; the French right wing and reserve numbered around 61,000 available troops.

Napoleon delayed his attack until about 2.30 p.m., which gave time for his army to deploy, but meant that there was limited time before night fell. Much of the fighting was centred on the crossing points over the Ligny stream in the various villages lying on its banks. The settlements of Ligny, Saint Amand, Saint Amand le Hameau and Wagnelee were fought over in ferocious combat, with both sides determined to gain control of the bridges.

Slowly Napoleon's attacks drew in Blücher's reserves until they were all engaged. The 72-year-old Blücher led one of the charges in person, but his horse was shot and fell on him. He was rescued by Major von Nostitz and taken in a semi-conscious condition from the field. While Blücher was out of action, his Chief of Staff, Lieutenant General August von Gneisenau, took over command.

A final thrust through Ligny village by Napoleon's Imperial Guard, supported by his heavy cavalry, finally broke through the Prussian centre and they were forced to retreat. However, as darkness was descending, Napoleon could not send out any troops in pursuit, allowing the Prussians to retire towards Wavre in pretty good order, where they could still co-operate with Wellington.

Having lost contact with the Prussians, French cavalry patrols were sent out the following morning and discovered some troops on the road to Namur, which led Napoleon to assume wrongly that the main Prussian army was in headlong retreat towards the Rhine and effectively out of the war.

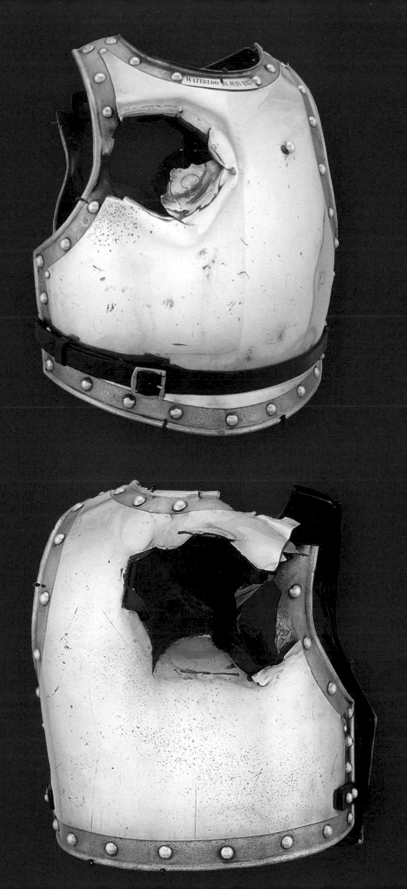

10

Cuirass of Carabinier François Fauveau

FRANÇOIS ANTOINE FAUVEAU was only 23 years old at the Battle of Waterloo. According to his service record, he joined the French 2nd Regiment of Carabiniers in May 1815, when he is described as having a long face, blue eyes, an aquiline nose, small mouth and brown hair. His height was 5ft 10in and he was a rookie in his regiment. At Waterloo he was struck full in the chest by a cannonball which passed straight through his body. His death would have been mercifully instant; he may well have seen the shot coming towards him for a split second but had no time to react. Many survivors of the battle claim that they saw cannonballs hurtling towards them, which luckily for them just missed them. There is one question over Fauveau's death: marriage records list him as getting married soon after Waterloo. It is possible that a sibling or a substitute took Fauveau's place in the battle to allow him to marry. It will probably remain a mystery.

Cuirassiers and carabiniers were the elite of the cavalry and usually had to be over 5ft 10in tall, quite a height for the time. They also had to have served in at least three campaigns and completed twelve years in the cavalry before they could join, although this requirement was dropped for the Waterloo campaign, when numbers were falling short. These troops were Napoleon's

Date of manufacture: c. 1814

Location: Musée de l'Armée, Paris, France

heavy cavalry, 'big men on big horses', the most feared troops on Napoleonic battlefields. When sent en masse against a weakened enemy, they could smash through to gain a decisive victory.

They were the only cavalrymen in Napoleon's army to wear protective body armour, a cuirass – a full breast and back plate connected by leather straps which covered the entire upper torso. They also wore an iron cap on their heads, with a fur turban wrapped around it and a copper crest surmounted by a horsehair mane. The cuirass worn at Waterloo had been brought into production in 1809; it was a rounded shape and slightly shorter than previous versions. The cuirass weighed approximately 28lb (13kg) and a fully equipped cuirassier weighed somewhere around 310lb (140kg), a heavy load for a horse. Because of this only the large Normandy horses were used for this role.

Helmet of a cuirassier officer.

The cuirass was reputed to be impervious to musket fire, but it was soon discovered that, although impenetrable to pistol fire, musket balls fired at close range would pass straight through. Even so, the preferred method for infantry to bring down a cuirassier with a musket was simply to shoot at his horse, which carried no form of protection at all. Unhorsed cuirassiers were useless; according to a number of eyewitnesses, a winded cuirassier thrown from his injured or dying horse would often find it impossible to raise himself from the ground in his armour if he landed on his back, not unlike an upturned turtle. A number describe how these cavalrymen were often finished off by a musket butt smashing their skull as they lay helplessly on the ground.

Napoleon had a total of some 4,500 heavy cavalry at Waterloo: two regiments of carabiniers and twelve regiments of cuirassiers, although one of these regiments fought at Waterloo without their cuirasses. There was only minimal difference between a carabinier and a cuirassier in regard to abilities or arms, but their uniforms were quite distinct. The cuirassiers wore a dark-blue tunic under a plain iron cuirass, the carabiniers wore a white tunic under a yellow brass-coloured cuirass (the colour was from a thin veneer of brass over the iron of the cuirass). Both were armed with a carbine or short musket, though this was rarely used in battle, and a long straight sword which was designed for stabbing rather than cutting.

The British soldiers had never had to face cuirassiers in Spain during the Peninsular War, where the terrain did not favour these heavy cavalry, and there was some apprehension and much discussion on how to deal with them at Waterloo. The cuirassiers' prowess and elite status was commonly mistaken by British soldiers, who often describe them as part of the cavalry of the Imperial Guard, which they were not.

The allied cavalry, armed only with swords, tried and succeeded with a number of strategies against their armoured opposite numbers. As the opponents closed towards each other on horseback, the allies had to ensure that they avoided the cuirassiers' sword points as they thrust them forward; if the allies had a curved sword, they could take a cut at the Frenchman's bridle or sword arm as he thrust forward so that he lost control; if the allies had a straight sword, they tried to thrust its point towards the Frenchman's throat and face. Beyond that, the tactic universally adopted seems to have been to stay in close to the cuirassier, where he could not gain the room to stab, and then to smash your hand guard into his face to knock him off his horse. If the opponents passed each other, the recommendation was to make a vicious back swipe at the back of the cuirassier's neck – if you got it right you would decapitate him.

II

King's Colour of 69th Foot

EVERY BATTALION OF the British army, including the King's German Legion, carried two sets of Colours; these flags were important to the battalions as rallying points, as the Eagles were to the French soldiers. The King's Colour consisted of a Union flag with the regimental number emblazoned on its centre. The second or Regimental Colour consisted of a plain flag of the regiment's distinguishing colour, which was always featured on the soldiers' collars and cuffs, and again emblazoned with the regimental number.

The carrying of the Colours was the privilege of the junior officers, known as ensigns, who carried swords, and protection for them was supplied by the Colour party. The privilege of protecting the Colours was a slightly dubious one, as the Colour also became the focus of attacks and the survival rate of ensigns in battle was not good.

It was a point of honour for regiments not to lose one of their Colours, but the 69th unfortunately lost one of theirs twice in just over a year. The first time was in March 1814, when they were forced to surrender at the storming of Bergen op Zoom. The second occasion was at Quatre Bras, when French cuirassiers surprised the regiment when they were not fully formed in square. Ensign George Ainslie carried the Regimental Colour

Date of production:
1814

Location:
Cardiff Castle, Cardiff, Wales

and was apparently knocked over by a horse. Volunteer Christopher Clarke, having caught the Colour, stubbornly held onto it, killing three cuirassiers and receiving twenty-three wounds before collapsing to the ground with the Colour under his body, thus saving it. Amazingly, Clarke survived, although he lost the use of one arm, and he gained a commission in the 42nd Foot for his bravery. The King's Colour, carried by Ensign Henry Keith, however, was lost in obscure circumstances in the same battle. The cavalry attack was sudden and the surprise so complete that few had time to react. It is strange to note that neither Ensign Ainslie nor Ensign Keith were apparently wounded at Quatre Bras in defence of their Colours.

A number of men of the 8th Cuirassiers variously claimed that they had captured the Colours of the 69th. In truth the Colours were probably seized by a group of cavalry, possibly including all of those named.

The Colours were apparently presented to Marshal Ney during the battle and somehow passed into the hands of General Xavier-Donzelot who commanded the 2nd Division of d'Erlon's corps in the Waterloo campaign.

In 1909, Captain Jeffcock, late of the 6th (Inniskilling) Dragoons, bought the 69th's Colours for £24 (about £1,500 in modern terms) at a market in Azay-le-Rideau in France, where they had been given away in lieu of an unpaid debt. They were eventually returned to the regiment and they now reside at the regimental museum in Cardiff Castle.

Two other Colours are known to have been lost at Waterloo: those of the 5th and 8th line battalions of the King's German Legion, both when they were ordered to advance separately in support of the garrison of La Haye Sainte Farm. The Colour of the 8th Line was, however, dropped when the officer carrying it was severely wounded, though it was not captured but soon recovered and returned to the regiment.

French claims of the capture of a number of other stands of Colours cannot be reconciled with the known facts and no other battalion Colours have come to light in France since.

A significant number of French flags were also captured during the Battle of Waterloo and a number of these have recently been rediscovered in the collection made by Sir Walter Scott at his home at Abbotsford.

However, these flags did not carry the same significance as the loss of the Eagle, as discussed later.

12

Statue of the Duke of Brunswick

by Ernst Julius Hahnel

Date of construction:
1874

Location:
Braunschweig or Brunswick, Germany

PRINCE FREDERICK WILLIAM, the Duke of Brunswick-Wolfenbüttel, was probably the most senior officer to die in the Waterloo campaign, and his loss was universally lamented.

The duke was born in Brunswick as the fourth son of Charles William Ferdinand, Duke of Brunswick-Lüneburg, and Princess Augusta of Great Britain. He was the cousin and brother-in-law of the Prince Regent, the future George IV. Frederick William joined the Prussian army in 1789 as a captain and participated in a number of battles against Revolutionary France. In 1802 he married Princess Marie Elisabeth of Baden. The couple had three children before Marie died of puerperal fever four days after giving birth to a stillborn daughter. In 1805, after his uncle, Frederick Augustus, Duke of Oels, had died childless, Frederick William inherited the Duchy of Oels, a small principality in Prussia.

In October 1806, Frederick William participated in the joint battles of Jena–Auerstedt as a major general. His father was a field marshal in the same battle, but he was wounded and later died. Frederick William inherited Brunswick-Wolfenbüttel, as his eldest brother had died childless only two months earlier, and both his second and third brothers were regarded as mentally unstable. After the defeat of Prussia in this war, his state remained under the control of France and was formally made a part of the short-lived Kingdom of Westphalia. Frederick William fled to the Grand Duchy of Baden, which had remained a sovereign state, where he lived for the next few years.

When the French war against Austria broke out in 1809, Frederick William used the opportunity to create a corps of partisans to fight the French. This corps was known as the Black Brunswickers because they wore black uniforms in mourning for their occupied country and the death of his father. He financed the corps independently by mortgaging his principality in Oels, but when Austria was rapidly defeated he made his way with his corps from Austrian Bohemia through the states of Saxony and Westphalia to the North Sea coast. He briefly managed to retake control of the city of Brunswick, or Braunschweig, in August 1809, which gained him the status of a local folk hero, but he then fled to England with his small corps to join forces with the British. His troops were taken into British pay and the duke was granted the rank of lieutenant general in the British army on 1 July 1809. The Brunswickers were sent to serve in Spain and Portugal with Wellington and the corps lost heavily in the Peninsular War (see item 28).

Frederick William returned to Brunswick in December 1813, after Prussia had ended French domination. When Napoleon returned from Elba in 1815, Frederick William raised fresh troops to go to war again. On the night of 15 June he attended the Duchess of Richmond's ball in Brussels and left it, apparently happy to have a chance to show off the fighting ability of his corps.

The Brunswickers were part of the reinforcements sent to help the Dutch division that was holding the crossroads at Quatre Bras on 16 June 1815. The Black Duke, as Frederick William was known, was seen during the fighting reassuring his inexperienced troops by walking up and down in front of them, calmly puffing on his pipe.

Later, as a mass of French infantry advanced up the main road, the duke led a charge by his uhlans (lancers), but they were beaten back. Struck by cannon fire at short range, the Brunswickers broke. At this point, the duke, who was busy reforming his troops, was hit by a musket ball, which passed through his hand and into his liver. He was retrieved by the men, who carried him back using their muskets as a stretcher, but he died shortly afterwards.

The Duke's final words, to his aide Major von Wachholtz, were: 'My dear Wachholtz, where is Olfermann?' Colonel Elias Olfermann was the duke's adjutant general; he assumed immediate command of the corps on his death.

I3 French camp kettle

IT IS OFTEN forgotten that for every battle a soldier is engaged in, he usually lives in camp peacefully for many months in between. Old soldiers on campaign would therefore use their experience to refine their kit, removing absolutely everything that was unnecessary and keeping as much room as possible for the essentials in their packs.

Officers of all nations demanded a higher level of comfort on campaign. Often they were given an allowance for a pack horse which could carry more luxurious

Date of manufacture:
c. 1815

Location:
Musée de l'Armée, Paris, France

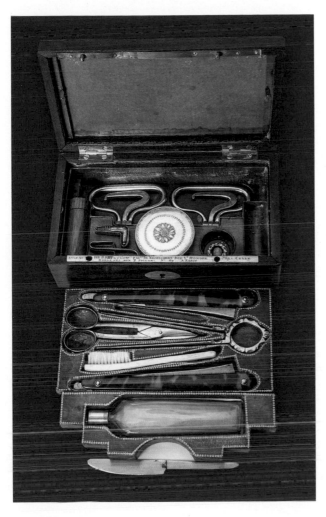

French néccessaire – a case containing all the essentials of camp life.

camp equipment, but the essential needs were still the same: food, protection from the weather and clean clothing. Tents, shaving equipment, crockery, cutlery and cooking implements were therefore specially designed to be compact and to fit into special containers which could be carried in pack saddles.

It was quite normal for officers to acquire a servant or two, either privately or supplied from within the regiment. The servant could draw rations, cook and clean for his master. Some officers indeed even had a cart, allowing them to take more equipment with them, including libraries to while away the long tedious hours when nothing happened. However, such luxury on campaign was often a cause of congestion on the roads following an army, severely hampering the free flow of supplies and reinforcements. It was therefore often necessary to order officers to leave such carts behind or threaten to have them burned if discovered. It has to be said, however, that many appear to have contrived to retain their luxuries.

14

The Waterloo map

THE DUKE OF Wellington ordered this map to be produced, covering the area of Belgium south of Brussels. A team of ten Royal Engineer officers, under the command of Lieutenant Colonel James Carmichael Smyth and Captain John Oldfield worked on it.

The sections of the map were drawn up using different qualities of paper, and each individual added different levels of detail as he thought necessary. One part was even drawn on inferior brown paper and is much less detailed; this may have been added in a rush as the campaign began. The map is an irregular shape, as the small maps were simply pasted together, not redrawn onto a overall large sheet, but its overall dimensions are around 4ft 5in x 3ft 3in (135cm x 99cm). The entire area of the map covers about 120 square miles, the scale of the map being approximately 4 inches to the mile. The area covered includes Halle, Genappe, Nivelles and the area where the Battle of Waterloo was fought.

With the sudden start of the campaign, the army marched from Brussels in haste and the map was required on campaign by the Duke of Wellington. Due to these time constraints, it was decided that the original sketches would be used. It is claimed that a fair copy of the map had previously been made and had already been

Date of production:
1815

Location:
Royal Engineers'
Museum, Chatham,
UK

61

presented to the Prince of Orange. However, this map cannot be found and it is not clear why a fair copy of an unfinished map would have been made; it is more likely that there was no fair copy.

The map was apparently held by Lieutenant Colonel John Waters, Assistant Adjutant General, who nearly lost it when he became involved in a melee at the Battle of Quatre Bras on 16 June. Waters was unhorsed during an assault by French cavalry and then spent the rest of the battle trying to evade capture. His horse had bolted, but by sheer luck Waters found it again, grazing quietly in a field, shortly after. The map was apparently used by the Duke of Wellington on 17 June to indicate where he would offer battle, this is shown by pencil lines on the ridge near La Haye Sainte. He then handed it to Sir William De Lancey, his quartermaster general, who made arrangements accordingly.

At the Battle of Waterloo, De Lancey carried the map on his person, reportedly in his jacket pocket. He was mortally wounded by a cannonball which struck him in the back. The map was apparently recovered by Captain Oldfield, who passed it on to Carmichael Smyth.

It has long been suggested that the dark area at the top of the map was the stain of De Lancey's blood. Claims that this was actually caused by a nineteenth-century attempt at conserving the map are certainly false as Sir Walter Scott described seeing the map at Paris in 1815, where it was already stained.

In 1846, Oldfield added an explanatory passage to the left of the map. His notes refer to the events surrounding the map's history. A transcript of the text on the map is as follows:

This plan consists of reconnoitering sketches of the position of Waterloo, and the adjacent Country, made by order of Lt. Colonel Carmichael Smyth, Commanding Royal Engineer in the Netherlands, by his Officers in the years 1814–15. One fair copy had been given to the H.R.H. The Prince of Orange, when Commander of the Forces, A second was ordered for his Grace the Duke of Wellington; but not being in a sufficient state of forwardness this original plan was sent to the Field when called for by His Grace on 16th June 1815. It was in custody of Lieut. Colonel Waters, R.E., lost and recovered in a melee with the French Cavalry at Quatre Bras.

On the 17th upon the Duke deciding upon retiring on Waterloo, His Grace called on the Commanding Engineer for the plan, who took it from Brigade Major Oldfield, Royal Engineers (to whom the custody had been transferred on his joining Head Quarters) and given to the Duke, by whom it was handed to His Quarter Master General, Lt. Col. Sir William De Lancey, K.C.B, with directions to place the troops in position; orders being at the same time given to Lt. Colonel Carmichael Smyth, relative to his own Department.

This Plan was on the person of Sir William De Lancey, when that Officer was killed;– it was recovered for Lt. Col. Carmichael Smyth by Brigade Major Oldfield, from Lt. Colonel Sir Charles V. Broke, D.Q.M. General at Cateau Cambresis on the advance upon Paris in June 1815; since which time it has been with the papers of Lt Colonel Sir James Carmichael Smyth, Baronet, CB;- KCH; K.M.J; K.S.N.J. Oldfield Colonel Royal Engineers 31st January 1846.

The map remained at the residence of Carmichael Smyth until his death in 1860. After this it was all but forgotten about. It resurfaced in 1910, when the Royal Engineers' Museum received a letter reporting the discovery of the map. A London-based bookseller had acquired it with a number of other maps and was willing to sell it. The museum did not have sufficient funds to purchase it at the time, so Major Harrison (a curator of the museum) bought it using his own money and lent it to the museum. In 1921, he gifted it to the museum.

15 British 1796 light cavalry sword

THE 1796 PATTERN curved light cavalry sword was the fearsome weapon used by all of the British and King's German Legion hussars and light dragoons (see item 74). This version was probably made by a local craftsman rather than a fine sword maker and carries a hand-engraved Latin motto on each side of the blade: *No me engaines sin honor* and *No me saives sin rason* – 'Do not draw me without honour' and 'Do not sheathe me without reason'.

Light cavalry, known under various names, such as light dragoons, hussars, chasseurs, chevau-leger, or uhlans, played a prominent role in the Napoleonic wars. Mounted on small, fast horses, they were ideal for use in skirmish battles and for reconnaissance, not unlike the role performed by light tanks today. They were also expected to perform as formed units on the battlefield, engaging other cavalry and charging infantry. However, their small lighter horses were no match for the horses of the heavy cavalry and they found tackling formed infantry a major problem. Indeed, during the French mass cavalry attacks there is good evidence to show

Date of manufacture:
c. 1815

Location:
Private collection

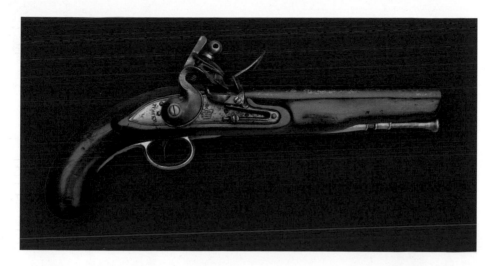

British 'tower' pistol.

that the British light cavalry did not perform well in the counter-charges designed to drive the French cavalry away.

Armed with a curved light cavalry sword that could cut through bone, but more often caused horrendous gashes which left large flaps of skin and muscle hanging down, the light cavalry also often carried cavalry pistols or short muskets known as carbines, which were rarely used in battle.

The main contribution of the British and Prussian light cavalry to the Battle of Waterloo was in fact the destruction they wrought within the already wavering ranks of the French army during the final phase of the battle, which undoubtedly helped to turn a retreat into a complete rout and prevented the French army from reforming.

16

The Blücher Mausoleum

THE NAME OF Field Marshal Gebhard von Blücher (pictured bottom, left) is synonymous with Waterloo. His dogged determination and drive to push his army across difficult country to join Wellington's army at Waterloo was a vital factor in the final victory. He was by no means a military genius, but his sheer determination and ability to recover from defeat made him a very effective leader.

Gebhard Leberecht von Blücher was born in Rostock in the Duchy of Mecklenburg-Schwerin, a Baltic port in northern Germany. His family had been landowners in the region since at least the thirteenth century, although his father was a military man. Gebhard began his military career at the age of 14, when he joined the Swedish army as a hussar during the war with Prussia in the Seven Years War. Having been captured in a skirmish with Prussian hussars, he was persuaded to join the Prussians instead.

He gained much experience of light cavalry work during this war. In peacetime, however, his exuberance led him into excesses of all sorts, such as the mock execution of a priest suspected of supporting the Polish uprisings. He was then passed over for promotion to major and wrote in a rude letter of resignation in 1773, to which King Frederick the Great replied: 'Cavalry Captain von Blücher can go to the devil.' Blücher settled

Date of construction:
1820

Location:
Krobielowice, Poland

down to farming on his family lands until the king died in 1786, when he was reinstated as a major in his regiment, and he had become its colonel by 1794. In 1801 he was promoted to lieutenant general.

Blücher was one of the leaders of the war party in Prussia in 1806 and he served in the disastrous Battle of Jena-Auerstedt. In the retreat of the Prussian army he commanded the rearguard and led a remnant of the Prussian army until his force was defeated at the Battle of Lübeck and he was compelled to surrender. He soon regained his freedom through exchange of prisoners.

After the war, Blücher was looked upon as the natural leader of the Patriot Party during the period of French domination of Prussia. In fact, he was a continual embarrassment to his government in its attempts to remain neutral, and in 1812 he expressed himself so openly that he was recalled from his post of military governor of Pomerania and effectively banished from court.

Following the disastrous losses of Napoleon's army during the Russian winter of 1812, Prussia joined the War of Liberation and Blücher was again placed in high command. He became commander-in-chief of the Army of Silesia, with August von Gneisenau as his principal staff officer and 90,000 men under his command. He was involved at the battles of Lutzen and Bautzen, and in the decisive defeat of Napoleon at the Battle of the Nations at Leipzig.

Blücher was made a field marshal in 1813. He pursued the French with his customary energy and was instrumental in pushing the war into France itself. He won a number of victories during this final campaign, but he also earned a reputation for resilience, immediately bouncing back from numerous defeats.

However, his health had been severely affected by the strain and he suffered a nervous breakdown, which included his believing that he had become pregnant by a French grenadier and was carrying an elephant! The allies continued the war and Napoleon was finally forced to abdicate, and Blücher recovered.

In gratitude for his victories in 1814, King Frederick William III of Prussia created Blücher Prince of

Wahlstatt. The king also awarded him estates near Krieblowitz in Lower Silesia, now in Poland, and a grand mansion in Berlin (which in 1930 became the United States embassy). Soon afterwards, Blücher visited England with the allied sovereigns; he was received with royal honours and cheered enthusiastically everywhere he went.

He briefly retired to Silesia, but the return of Napoleon soon called him back to service. He was put in command of the Army of the Lower Rhine, with Gneisenau as his Chief of Staff again. The Prussians sustained a serious defeat at the Battle of Ligny on 16 June 1815, in the course of which the old field marshal lay trapped under his dead horse and was repeatedly ridden over by the cavalry. He was unable to resume command for some hours, and in his absence Gneisenau ordered a retreat on Wavre. After bathing his wounds in brandy, Blücher rejoined his army and promised Wellington that at least two corps would join him at Waterloo. He led his army on the march along muddy paths, arriving at Waterloo in the late afternoon. The battle was hanging in the balance, but Blücher's army intervened with decisive effect, his vanguard drawing off part of Napoleon's reserves. With victory, Blücher drove his troops on all night, giving the French no rest or any opportunity to reform.

Blücher remained in Paris for a few months, but his age and infirmity compelled him to retire to his estates. He died at Krieblowitz on 12 September 1819, aged 76. After his death, an imposing mausoleum was built for his remains.

From 1937 to 1945 under the Nazis, Krieblowitz was renamed as Blüchersruh – Blücher's resting place. The mausoleum was desecrated by rampaging Soviet troops towards the end of the Second World War, and the area was given to Poland in 1945. The mausoleum remains an empty crumbling shell, but the field marshal's actual remains are buried in nearby Sośnica (Schosnitz), having been taken there for safety by a Polish priest after the fall of communism in Poland.

17 Silver plate

from Napoleon's breakfast service used at Le Caillou

LE CAILLOU, MEANING Pebble Farm, was owned by a farmer named Boucquéau in 1815. It was chosen as headquarters for Napoleon the night before the Battle of Waterloo and the Boucquéaus and their furniture were evicted.

The house has subsequently seen quite a few transformations and does not look as it did then. On the morning of 19 June 1815 the Prussian troops destroyed the house by setting fire to it and it remained nothing more than a shell for a few years, but was bought and turned into a tavern in 1818. Purchased by a local architect in the 1860s, it was turned into a villa and from then on its appearance was much as it is today.

In 1905 the property was sold to the Countess Villegas, who later married the historian Lucien Laudy, who began to form a collection of military memorabilia from the battle and erected an ossuary for bones discovered by the local farmers. This military collection forms the basis of the collection held there today, although, because of the fire, claims that the furniture is original must be treated with some suspicion.

Napoleon apparently dined alone that night but was upset by the talk of a number of senior officers in the adjoining room on the coming battle. Napoleon is said to have burst into the room, exclaiming loudly, 'A battle! Gentlemen! Are you sure you know what a battle is? Between a battle won and a battle lost, there are empires, kingdoms, the world – or nothing.'

At breakfast, Napoleon sat down with his senior officers, apparently in a very good mood. However the atmosphere soon changed. First General Drouot requested a few more hours' delay before the battle to allow the cannon to move into position in the heavy mud, which was reluctantly granted. Marshal Soult, who had fought Wellington in Spain, then suggested that Napoleon should manoeuvre rather than attack Wellington's army head-on in a prepared position. This caused Napoleon to snap back, 'Because Wellington has beaten you, you think he is a great general. I tell you Wellington is a bad general, the English are bad troops and this affair will be no more difficult than eating one's breakfast.'

In the walled orchard adjoining the house, a simple monument can be found noting their presence there throughout the battle of the 1st Battalion 1st Regiment Chasseurs of the Imperial Guard who formed Napoleon's guard.

Date of manufacture:
c. 1815

Location:
Goodwood House, Chichester, UK

18 Map of the current and proposed Preservation Area

IN THE RUN up to the centenary celebration of the Battle of Waterloo planned for June 1915, it was decided that it was necessary to protect the site of the battle before a mass of building work obliterated it forever. Brussels had expanded greatly during the century, as had the villages of Waterloo, Plancenoit and Braine l'Alleud and there was no time to waste before these villages expanded across the main areas of the battlefield. Luckily, the Walloon regional government passed a law on 26 March 1914 to protect the area which had seen the majority of the fighting between Wellington's allied army and Napoleon's French army. It is fortunate that the law was passed before the event, as the beginning of the First World War precluded any celebrations happening at all. This protected area is marked in purple on the map.

It should not be imagined that the battlefield had not already changed significantly. The construction of the Lion Mound had radically altered the allied ridge, Hougoumont Wood had been levelled and a monastery built near Papelotte and Braine l'Alleud had grown to cover most of the allied reserve areas on the right. To all intents and purposes, though, the main area of fighting was luckily still largely recognisable.

However, the area around Plancenoit where the Prussians fought was not protected by the Act. Although the village has grown significantly, it still retains many of its original buildings and has not entirely lost its character.

In time for the 200th anniversary of the battle the Walloon government intends to expand the protected

Date of production:
2014

Location:
Waterloo, Belgium

area to cover the areas of the French reserves, Plancenoit and around Mont St Jean and the left wing of the allied ridge. The proposed extension of the protection area is marked in blue on the map.

The aim is to increase the protected area from the original 1,346 acres to an area covering 2,948 acres. It is hoped thereby to preserve the routes and movements of the various armies and to protect the landscape and its agricultural heritage.

Let us hope that the extension to the protection area is agreed.

19 Forest of Soignes

THE FOREST OF Soignes or Sonian Forest (in Dutch: Zoniënwoud, in French: Forêt de Soignes) is a 10,900-acre (44km²) forest that lies immediately to the south of Brussels. This ancient woodland is first mentioned in the Middle Ages. Around 1815 the area of the wood was still nearly 25,000 acres (100 km²), but felling has since diminished its area.

Even before Waterloo the forest had contracted rapidly when Napoleon ordered 22,000 oaks to be cut down to build the Boulogne flotilla intended for the invasion of England. King William I of the Netherlands subsequenly continued to harvest the woods, and the forest was reduced to its current size by about 1830.

Wellington has been severely criticised by many, including Napoleon, for offering battle with a great forest in his immediate rear, which would have made it difficult for his army, if defeated, to retire in an organised retreat. His apologists claim that the high forest canopy prevented much undergrowth from growing, and thus easy movement through the forest would have

Date of origin:
Unknown – ancient woodland

Location:
South of Brussels, Belgium

been possible. Modern photographs of the forest seem to support this argument, but eyewitness reports from the time of the battle indicate that riders who struck off from the main Brussels road and attempted to cut through the forest found it nigh-on impossible to do so because of obstructions, boundary markers and flooded streams.

In Wellington's defence, a survey of maps produced in the thirty years prior to the battle, show that there were at least eight roads or track-ways other than the main *chaussée* leading through the forest towards Brussels. It would seem that the duke planned on using all of these routes to retire rapidly, comfortable that the pursuing French cavalry could not outflank them by riding through the forest. Proof that Wellington planned to utilise these roads is the fact that he ordered his engineers to fortify the village of Merbe Braine in the rear of his right wing. This village protected the entrance to a number of the roads running through the forest and could have been held by his rearguard for a considerable period as his army passed through in their rear.

Rights to a considerable portion of the forest in the neighbourhood of Waterloo were assigned in 1815 to the Duke of Wellington, whose heirs still retain the title of Prince of Waterloo in the Dutch nobility, the present duke receiving the equivalent of about £86,000 per annum from his Belgian properties. Recent attempts by the Belgian opposition to rescind this agreement have been thwarted.

The forest served for a long period as an exclusive hunting ground for the nobility, but today is open to the general public and is a very popular place to escape the stresses of city life.

20 Wellington's headquarters

ON THE NIGHT of 17 June 1815, the Duke of Wellington and his Staff took up residence at the headquarters hastily set up at the old Bodenghien inn. This building, opposite Waterloo Church, was witness to many incidents throughout the four-day campaign.

On 16 June the duke and his Staff breakfasted here en route to Quatre Bras, where a desperate battle was fought between Marshal Ney's wing of the French army and Wellington's troops in a battle of encounter where troops were simply thrown into the fray as soon as they arrived.

The duke returned here on the night of the 17th to write his orders for the army for the following morning. Wellington and his Staff left at dawn to command

Date of construction:
1705

Location:
Waterloo, Belgium

his troops at the Battle of Waterloo and it was only late that night that the duke returned, almost alone, to find food prepared to welcome his Staff back. Few came to claim their share; most had been wounded or killed. As Wellington put his faithful horse Copenhagen into the stables here and gently patted his rump the horse let out a most violent kick, which just missed the duke.

It was here that Wellington sat down at his desk to begin writing his despatch to the Prince Regent announcing the victory. Too tired to complete it, he retired for a few brief hours' sleep but was awoken by Dr Hume to announce the death of so many senior officers, including his aide-de-camp Alexander Gordon, who had just died of his wound in an adjoining room.

Wellington left here on the morning of 19 June and proceeded to Brussels, where he completed his despatch.

The building has been made into the Wellington Museum, containing many artefacts of the Waterloo campaign in its fourteen rooms, including the very bed in which Gordon died (see item 55).

2I Remains of a shrapnel shell

APART FROM THE rocket, which was probably the most frightening weapon in the battle, the most effective and destructive weapon at Waterloo was undoubtedly the 'spherical case' shot, more often colloquially known as the shrapnel shell.

Henry Shrapnel of Midway Manor in Bradford on Avon (1761–1842) was an artillery officer whose name has entered the English language as the inventor of this shell. In 1784, Lieutenant Shrapnel began developing a long-range, anti-personnel weapon. At the time artillery could defend themselves from infantry or cavalry attack by using 'canister shot', which involved loading a tin or canvas container filled with small iron or lead balls instead of the usual cannonball. When fired, the container burst open at the muzzle, giving the effect of an over-sized shotgun. The balls spread further as the distance grew from the barrel; canister was only really effective up to 200 yards.

Shrapnel's innovation was to delay the dispersal of the lead balls by using a fuse. His shell was a hollow cast-iron sphere filled with a mixture of balls and powder, with a crude fuse. If the fuse was set correctly the shell

Date of manufacture:
c. 1815

Location:
Private collection

would break open above the intended target, releasing its contents (of musket balls). The shrapnel balls would carry on with the remaining velocity of the shell. The explosive charge in the shell was to be just enough to break the casing rather than to scatter the shot in all directions. This invention increased the effective range of canister shot to about 1,000 yards.

Initial designs suffered from the potentially catastrophic problem that friction between the shot and black powder during the high acceleration down the gun bore could sometimes cause premature ignition of the powder. It was not until 1803 that the British artillery adopted the shrapnel shell, but then did so with great enthusiasm.

The first recorded use of shrapnel by the British was in 1804 against the Dutch at Fort Amsterdam in Surinam. In 1814, the British government recognised Shrapnel's contribution by awarding him £1,200 a year (worth about £60,000 today) for life.

At Waterloo, the shell's most noted contribution was when used against massed troop formations and is credited with ending the first attempt on Hougoumont almost single handedly when a few well-aimed shots struck large numbers down and created consternation in the French columns, causing them to retire.

Shrapnel was appointed to the office of colonel commandant of the Royal Artillery in 1827 and he had risen to the rank of lieutenant general by 1837. He lived at Peartree House, near Peartree Green, Southampton, from about 1835 until his death in 1842.

The 'spherical case shot' was not officially titled the 'shrapnel shell' until June 1852, on order of a government select committee, some ten years after the inventor's death. The term 'shrapnel' is now often incorrectly used to refer to fragments produced by *any* explosive weapon.

22

Shako of the Coldstream Guards

THIS VERY RARE example of a shako worn by a soldier of the light company, bearing the regimental plate of the Coldstream Guards and the bugle-horn insignia that denoted the light infantry companies (see also item 33), is a direct relic of the intense fighting during the Battle of Waterloo around the large farmhouse of Château d'Hougoumont.

On the evening of 17 June the light companies of the four Guard battalions present at Waterloo were sent down from the ridge to occupy the farmstead and were ordered to make it ready for defence. The two companies of the 1st Guards under Lieutenant Colonel Alexander, Lord Saltoun, were posted in the orchard, whilst the light companies of the Coldstream and 3rd Guards battalions under Lieutenant Colonel James Macdonell prepared to defend the farmstead, as well as manufacturing firing steps and stockpiling ammunition.

During the early phases of the battle, Macdonell's companies fought outside the farmstead, whilst only the Nassau battalion under Major Busgen defended the farm complex itself. As the attacks on Hougoumont intensified, these companies retired within the farm and took over the defence of the château and the northern gate. At around 1 p.m. the French attack advanced along the western side of the farm and actually reached

Date of manufacture:
1815

Location:
Musée de l'Armée, Brussels, Belgium

81

the northern gate. Sous Lieutenant Legros suceeded in breaking open the wooden gate using an axe, and around thirty men managed to enter the northern court-yard. Macdonell led a counter-attack which managed to shut the gates again and the French men trapped inside surrendered or were killed.

The south gate and gardener's house at Hougoumont.

Additional companies of the Guards battalions were added to the defence as the battle progressed, and an ammunition resupply was accomplished by a very brave driver of the Royal Waggon Train named Joseph Brewster (or Brewer), who drove his wagon in under fire; he was later transferred to the 3rd Foot Guards as a corporal. At around 3 p.m. the French tried a new tactic, firing incendiaries to set the farm ablaze. This succeeded in setting fire to the château. As the château burned down, the French managed to break in by a small side door on the west side of the farm and a dozen or more men got into the southern courtyard. These men were met by the Nassau troops, supported by the British Guardsmen escaping from the burning château. All of the Frenchmen who could not retire

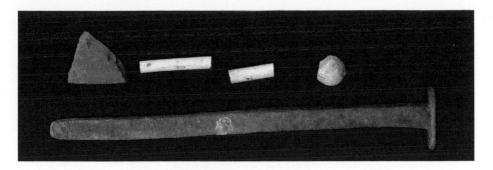

Nail from the north gate, roof tile, musket ball and pieces of clay pipe found at Hougoumont.

were apparently killed, except for a single drummer boy. Those who managed to escape took a handful of Nassau prisoners with them. The Frenchmen previously captured in the northern courtyard took this break-in as a signal to attempt to break out and support this breach. They were hunted down and summarily put to death.

There is a claim that the southern gate was also broken open by a cannonball, but no French infantry were able to take advantage of this and enter before the gates were closed again and barricaded.

After the battle, the Duke of Wellington wrote: 'You may depend upon it, no troops could have held Hougoumont but the British, and only the best of them', which completely ignores the efforts of the Nassau troops and others throughout the day.

When a request was sent to Wellington to name the bravest man at Waterloo by a Reverend John Norcross, rector of Framlingham, Suffolk, who wished to grant an annuity of £10 per year (about £425 in today's terms) on the nominee, the duke nominated Corporal James Graham of the light company of the Coldstream Guards, for his efforts in the 'closing of the gates' incident and the saving of his brother from a fire in the great barn. The annuity was only paid for two years before the reverend was declared bankrupt.

Hougoumont is currently undergoing a major refurbishment paid for jointly by subscriptions and British government finance. The intention is to turn the farm complex into a memorial to the British troops who fought at Waterloo.

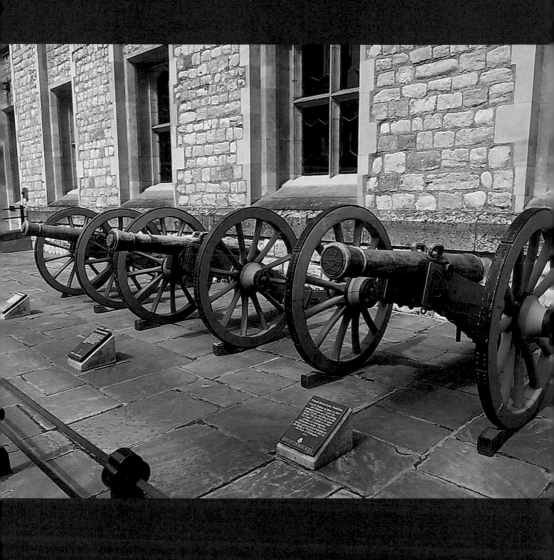

23

French cannon captured at Waterloo

THREE FRENCH 6-POUNDER cannon captured at the Battle of Waterloo now stand proudly outside Waterloo Barracks in the Tower of London. It is sometimes claimed that, as a precursor to Comte d'Erlon's corps' attack on Wellington's left wing, a grand battery of around eighty cannon was formed to weaken Wellington's infantry line. But everything regarding this battery is still a point of debate: its size, which units formed it and even where it stood.

The distance from the crest of the allied ridge to the slight rise which formed the front line of the French army – on which the track from Belle Alliance ran to Papelotte – was around 1,100 yards (1,000m), the maximum effective range for artillery. In the shallow valley between these two ridges, a small rise can be found just south of La Haye Sainte which, it is claimed, was used by the French artillery, as this brought the range down to a much more effective 660 yards (600m). Recent claims that the artillery moved forward onto this ridge, unprotected by infantry or cavalry, are certainly very wide of the mark. It is also certain that the British troops had never faced such a large battery before and although many memoirs talk of the heavy cannonade, none talks of seeing a long continuous line of cannon in their front.

Date of manufacture:
1813–14

Location:
Tower of London, London, UK

French sources confirm that their batteries were initially sited on the ridge where the trackway was and that the batteries were positioned in front of their own divisions as would be expected. The artillery of d'Erlon's corps, numbering forty-six cannon, was employed along this front, together with the reserve cannon supplied by Reille's and Lobau's corps, totalling a further sixteen cannon. The Imperial Guard reserve of artillery was also ordered to join, but did not unlimber to fire. Therefore the number of cannon firing on the British left wing at that time numbered sixty-two cannon.

When d'Erlon's infantry began to march towards Wellington's ridge, the corps' artillery of forty-six cannon moved forwards with them and established themselves as individual batteries along the central ridge. The reserve cannon remained in their original positions, the Guard artillery still remaining silent.

When the British heavy cavalry destroyed d'Erlon's corps, the Scots Greys rode on for the cannon, cutting down the gunners and drivers and reputedly effectively putting as many as forty cannon out of action for the remainder of the day. As the total number of cannon

Two French cannon and two howitzers captured at Waterloo, now at Royal Chelsea Hospital.

on the forward ridge only numbered forty-six, and as these were spread over a long distance, it is safe to say that the number of guns disabled must have been less than twenty. Those that survived retired to their original position.

At the end of the battle, over 150 French cannon were captured on the battlefield or abandoned during the ensuing rout and allied units claimed them by chalking their regimental numbers on the barrels as they passed. However, Colonel Sir Augustus Frazer, who had commanded the British Horse Artillery at Waterloo, rode out in the early hours of 20 June, picking up groups of straggling artillery men and horses as they went, but found very few cannon to collect. In something of a panic, not wanting to be the man to inform the Duke of Wellington that they had lost the captured cannon, he rode on to Genappe, to find over 200 French cannon parked up under Prussian guards. The Prussians had methodically collected together all of the abandoned cannon they could find during the previous day. The Prussian officer in charge was very accommodating, though. Frazer proved that the cannon had been captured by Wellington's troops by showing the Prussian a return that had been made out of the guns captured at Waterloo and by pointing out the still-obvious chalk marks of the regiments, and then he was allowed to repossess over 160 guns. The Prussians retained a further fifty they found abandoned in the log jam of vehicles at Genappe, and even more were captured on the road to Paris.

24 General Picton's hat

LIEUTENANT GENERAL SIR Thomas Picton was the most senior British officer to die at Waterloo. Picton was respected for his courage and loathed for his irritable nature. He is chiefly remembered for his exploits under Wellington in the Peninsular War. He was killed fighting at the Battle of Waterloo, during a crucial bayonet charge in which his division attempted to halt d'Erlon's corps' attack against the allied centre left.

He was born in Haverfordwest, Pembrokeshire on 24 August 1758. In 1771 he obtained a commission in the 12th Regiment of Foot, but he did not join until two years later. The regiment was then stationed at Gibraltar, where Picton remained until he was made captain in January 1778, at which point he returned to Britain. After living on his father's estate for nearly twelve years, he went out to the West Indies in 1794 as an aide-de-camp and gained a captaincy in the 17th Foot. Shortly

Date of manufacture: c. 1815

Location: National Army Museum, London, UK

afterwards he was promoted to major in the 58th Foot and became governor of Trinidad.

In 1810, he was appointed to command a division in Spain. Wellington recognised his fighting qualities, but once described Picton as 'a rough foul-mouthed devil as ever lived'. For the remaining years of the Peninsular War, Picton was one of Wellington's principal subordinates. He fought at Busaco, Fuentes d'Onoro and the sieges of Ciudad Rodrigo and Badajoz. He was himself wounded at the terrible storming of Badajoz Castle but would not leave the ramparts. His wound, and an attack of fever, compelled him to return to Britain to recuperate, but he reappeared at the front again in April 1813. While in Britain he had been invested with the Knight of the Order of the Bath and in June he was made a lieutenant general in the army. He then fought at Vitoria, the Pyrenees, Orthes and Toulouse. When Napoleon returned from Elba, Picton, at Wellington's request, accepted a high command in the Anglo-Dutch army.

Picton attended the Duchess of Richmond's ball that was held on 15 June; he was wounded at Quatre Bras the next day, but concealed his wound and retained command of his troops. At Waterloo two days later, he commanded the 5th Infantry Division. When Napoleon ordered Comte d'Erlon's corps to attack the allied left wing at around 1.30 p.m., Picton launched a bayonet charge on the advancing French columns. While repulsing the attack he was shot through the temple by a musket ball.

Family tradition claims that Picton had fought the battle wearing civilian clothes, including a top hat, because his luggage had not arrived, or that he rode in his nightshirt and top hat because he had overslept. These tales are perhaps fanciful, but it does appear that one of Picton's eccentricities was a dislike of wearing uniform and that he habitually wore mufti on active service. The hat pictured was one of those regularly worn by Picton.

His body was brought home to London, and buried in the family vault at St George's, Hanover Square.

25

Jacket of a Life Guard

THE ILLUSTRATION SHOWS the undress jacket of a Life Guard, as was worn on active service by officers and other ranks in place of the heavily laced dress jacket worn on ceremonial occasions.

The Household Cavalry was usually stationed in England to protect the king's person and rarely served abroad. However, it was sent to serve in Spain with the Duke of Wellington in 1812 and fought at the Battle of Vitoria in 1813.

At Waterloo the Household Cavalry Brigade, commanded by Major General Lord Edward Somerset, consisted of two squadrons of the Royal Horse Guards (of which Wellington was colonel), along with two squadrons each of the two regiments of the Life Guards and four squadrons of the King's Dragoon Guards, amounting to 1,350 cavalrymen in total. The brigade stood to the right of the main Brussels road, just in front of the farm of Mont St Jean, in reserve behind the infantry. Here they remained, only suffering from the occasional cannonball coming over the ridge.

At around 1.30 p.m. the Comte d'Erlon's corps marched against the allied left wing. This was supported by a brigade of cuirassiers who rode up the slope to the west of La Haye Sainte. The cuirassiers rode over a Hanoverian battalion which had been intended to

Date of manufacture:
c. 1815

Location:
National Army Museum, London, UK

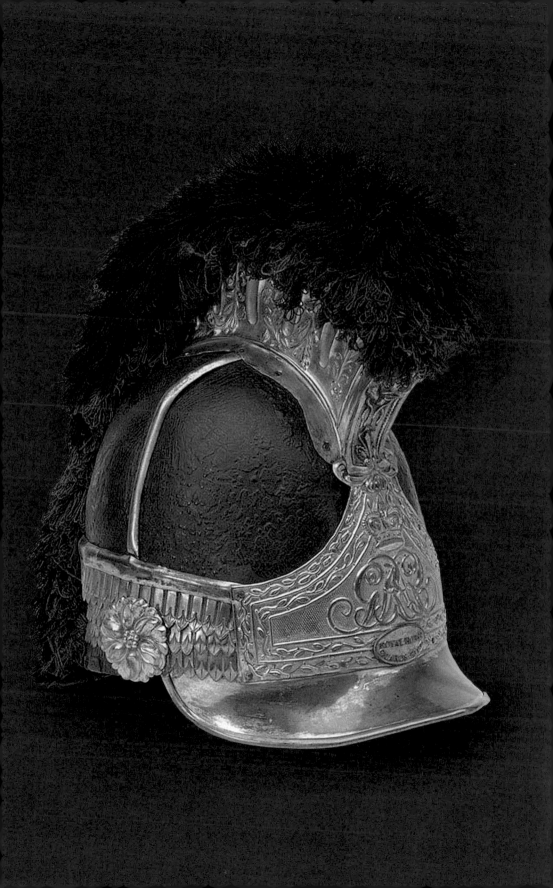

reinforce the defence of the farm, scattering it, and then continued towards the ridge. As the cuirassiers neared the crossroads, they threatened the 95th Rifles, who fled for safety, some not returning to the fight that day.

Lord Uxbridge now launched the Household Cavalry Brigade in a swift counter-attack, catching the cuirassiers in their flank and driving them back down the slope. Here they also drove into the French infantry that was trying to capture La Haye Sainte, forcing them back, and it is reported that Lieutenant Tathwell Baker Tathwell captured the Eagle of the 55th Régiment de Ligne (see item 26), but he was soon captured and the Eagle retrieved. The lieutenant effected his escape only two days later.

The Household Cavalry were then driven back by a counter-attack from a large French cavalry force, including lancers, who had a great advantage during such confused close combat. The Life Guards bore the brunt of this, while the Royal Horse Guards were used as a reserve and covered the Household Cavalry's retreat to the ridge.

Returning to their original position, the Household Cavalry were involved in numerous counter-moves during the mass French cavalry attacks against the allied right wing between 3 and 6 p.m. Sadly depleted by losses during these charges and the constant cannon fire, they eventually formed only a thin line, which was placed hard up behind the infantry line to encourage them to continue to stand.

Around this time Major General Sir Hussey Vivian, commander of the 6th Cavalry Brigade, arrived from the left wing and asked Lord Edward Somerset where his brigade was. Somerset apparently simply pointed to the piles of dead men and horses littering the field around him.

Captain Wililam
Tyrwhitt Drake's
helmet, Royal Horse
Guards.

The Household Cavalry was now an exhausted and spent force and could not assist in any meaningful way in the final advance after the defeat of the Imperial Guard.

26

Eagle of 45ème Régiment de Ligne

THE EAGLE WAS the most prized possession of each regiment of the French army. Every battalion in a regiment carried a flag, but only the first carried the Eagle on top of the flagpole. Issued personally by Napoleon to the regiments at the great meeting known as the Champ de Mai just before the Waterloo campaign commenced, this symbol was defended to the death during the battle. Two Eagles were captured at Waterloo – the 45ème and the 105ème – a difficult and rare achievement, indeed; during the entire Peninsular War only eight were taken by British forces.

Sergeant Charles Ewart serving with the Scots Greys, captured the Eagle of the 45ème Régiment de Ligne at the Battle of Waterloo. He was born near Kilmarnock in 1769 and enlisted in the regiment at the age of 20 and became a well-respected soldier, serving as fencing master. A heavily built man, reported as between 6ft and 6ft 4in tall and 'of Herculean strength', he was an accomplished rider.

At Waterloo, the Greys were part of the Union Brigade, which made a decisive charge to destroy the Comte d'Erlon's corps which was close to defeating Wellington's left wing. The Greys surprised the French infantry and broke through the column. In the confusion that followed, the 45ème was destroyed as an

Date of manufacture:
1815

Location:
Museum of the Royal Scots Dragoon Guards, Edinburgh Castle, Scotland

organised unit, and Sergeant Ewart gained the Eagle in close fighting with a number of Frenchmen. He recalled:

> One made a thrust at my groin, I parried him off and cut him down through the head. A lancer came at me, I threw the lance off by my right side and cut him through the chin and upwards through the teeth. Next, a foot soldier fired at me and then charged me with his bayonet, which I also had the good luck to parry, and then I cut him down through the head.

Ewart was rewarded with an ensigncy in the 5th Veteran Battalion in 1816, and left the army when this unit was disbanded in 1821. He was hailed as a hero and travelled the country giving speeches.

He retired on full pay and lived out his final years at Davyhulme, near Manchester, and died in 1846. His grave was eventually paved over and forgotten for many years, only being uncovered in the 1930s, when he was reburied by the Royal Scots Greys on the esplanade of Edinburgh Castle in 1938.

The capture of the Eagle of the 105ème Régiment de Ligne has been and still is the subject of great controversy regarding who actually took it. This argument revolves around two claimants: Captain Alexander Kennedy Clark and Corporal Francis Stiles (or Styles), both of the 1st (Royal) Regiment of Dragoons, which was another regiment in the Union Brigade.

A week after Waterloo, Captain Kennedy Clark wrote to his sister: 'I had the honour to stab the bearer of the 45th battalion of infantry and take the eagle which is now in London. It is a very handsome blue silk flag with a large gilt eagle on top of the pole with the wings spread.' This statement contains two very clear mistakes: the Eagle captured by the Royals was that of the 105ème, and the flag attached was a tricolour, not simply blue.

Kennedy Clark had been wounded at Waterloo and in July 1815, whilst he was still recovering, he became increasingly anxious that his deed at Waterloo had been overlooked and therefore wrote to his colonel requesting his help.

A regimental investigation was held and statements from privates Anderson and Wilson, both of whom had been closely involved in the struggle, were submitted. Anderson's statement was to the effect that he:

> was to the left of Captain Clark when he stabbed the officer. He and the officer fell and the eagle fell across the heads of his and Captain Clark's horse and against that of Corporal Stiles. Captain Clark called out twice together 'Secure the colour'. Corporal Stiles seized it and carried off the eagle to the rear. Anderson was wounded soon after and rode part of the way from the field with the corporal.

Wilson's description of the events was that he:

> was about to quit the field when he heard Captain Clark call out to secure the colour and turned about to assist in taking it. He was a horse's length to the right of Captain Clark when he stabbed the officer who carried it. The colour and the eagle fell against the neck of Corporal Stiles' horse who snatched it up and galloped off to the rear.

Corporal Stiles wrote to his former troop commander at Waterloo, Lieutenant George Gunning, in January 1816 to garner his support. Gunning later wrote:

> I saw an eagle among a small body. I told corporal Styles to secure it, and led the men on to the attack. At this moment I saw no officer near me. I killed the French officer who commanded the party, whose sword passed between my arm and my body at the moment my sword passed through his left breast. He was a fine looking, elegant man; his last words were 'Vive l'Empereur'. The prisoners said he was the commanding officer of the 105th regi-

Eagle of 105ème
Régiment de Ligne.

ment. It was the work of a moment. I saw the eagle in the hands of corporal Styles and I ordered him to leave the field, and not give up the eagle until he had a proper receipt for it at headquarters from one of the Duke of Wellington's personal staff.

Following this investigation Stiles was promoted, first to sergeant and then to ensign in the 6th West India Regiment.

In his despatch to Lord Bathurst dated 19 June, Wellington makes mention of the capture of three Eagles. He had opportunity to correct this at Brussels but did not do so, apparently in the clear belief that three Eagles had been captured. Although this was later proved incorrect, it is possible that another was captured for at least a period of time. There were persistent claims that Lieutenant Tathwell Baker Tathwell of the Royal Horse Guards also captured an Eagle during this charge, but subsequently lost it when he was captured. Colonel Bro of the French lancers claims to have recaptured an Eagle (although it is unclear whether it was the same one), and indeed the regimental history of the 55ème Régiment de Ligne, which was engaged in attacking La Haye Sainte at this time, states that they temporarily lost their Eagle. The circumstantial evidence does tend towards this being the third Eagle reported as captured to the Duke of Wellington, but it was recovered by the French.

27 British 9-pounder cannon

THE 9-POUNDER CANNON was by 1815 the standard artillery piece for the British army and is credited with being a major factor in the allied victory. However, claims that the 9-pounder was introduced to give the artillery greater firepower in the run-up to Waterloo is not an entirely accurate assessment.

The British army had used 12-pounders in the field as early as the turn of the century, and at least one battery of these heavy guns had served with Wellington in the Peninsular War. These heavier-calibre guns matched the French 12-pounders for weight of fire, but the rugged terrain and poor roads of Spain, the extra weight of carrying a large reserve of 12-pound shot and the lack of sufficient horsepower needed to transport it caused

Date of manufacture:
1812–15

Location:
Sandhurst, UK

the 12-pounders to be slowly phased out in preference to lighter and more manoeuvrable 6-pounders.

During the Waterloo campaign, the horse artillery still initially retained their 6-pounders but, now that they were in the flatter country of Belgium, with better road systems and better quality horses available, thoughts of ramping up the calibre of the artillery re-emerged. Wellington was also well aware of Napoleon's use of large batteries to soften up his opposition before launching his attacks. Here the age-old problem of matching the firepower of the French 12-pounders became more of an issue again.

Changing the 6-pounders in the batteries, not to 12-pounders, but to 9-pounders, was a very practical choice. The 9-pounders could carry nearly 25 per cent more rounds than the 12-pounder, with the same number of horses, and thus would be much more effective in a the prolonged battle that was anticipated.

The decision to change the size of the guns is usually credited to Lieutenant Colonel Sir Augustus Frazer who commanded the Royal Horse Artillery at Waterloo. However, the evidence actually points to the decision having been made by the Earl of Musgrave, Master General of the Ordnance, who instigated the change.

After the artillery reorganisation of 1803, the French usually only used 6- and 12 pounders in the field. Indeed, of a total of 178 French guns deployed at Waterloo, only 36 of the cannon were 12-pounders and half of these were with the Imperial Guard and retained in reserve. It can therefore be seen that the allied artillery, carrying some sixty 9-pounders out of a total of 141 cannon, actually outgunned the French gun for gun. The decision to upgrade many of the horse artillery troops to 9-pounders from the old 6-pounders just before the battle was a huge and possibly decisive improvement.

28 Brunswick shako

THIS HEADGEAR, BECAUSE of its quality and the metal chin scales, would seem to indicate that it was worn by an officer in the Brunswick Hussars. The black uniform and skull and cross bones on their badges denoted mourning for the Duke of Brunswick mortally wounded at the Battle of Auerstedt in 1806 and their desire for revenge on the French.

After the defeat of Austria in 1809, his son, the present Duke of Brunswick, had marched his force of about 2,000 men towards the north German ports and succeeded in rendezvousing with the Royal Navy at Elsfleth on the River Weser (see item 12). They were initially taken to Heligoland and then on to the Isle of Wight, where they reorganised and were incorporated into the British army.

The Brunswick-Oels troops initially performed well in Spain and Portugal under Wellington but as the battalions suffered casualties they were replenished with a mixed bag of recruits, including many ex-prisoners of war. They thus rapidly gained a reputation for high rates of desertion as these ex-prisoners of war took

Date of manufacture:
1812–15

Location:
Private collection

Brunswick Waterloo medal.

the first opportunity to escape, and they became renowned as scavengers who would even eat dogs.

The Brunswick troops left British service with the end of the war in 1814 and returned home. Here, they were reformed and all alien recruits still present were paid off. The Duke of Brunswick increased the size of his corps by wholesale recruitment to participate with the allies against Napoleon.

The Brunswick Corps fought as an independent unit during the campaign and numbered some 5,000 infantry and 2,000 cavalry and sixteen cannon. The corps formed part of Wellington's reserve and was stationed near Brussels.

The Brunswickers marched to Quatre Bras on 16 June and generally fought well alongside Picton's division in holding off the heavy French attacks, but during one attack the Duke of Brunswick was mortally wounded and died soon after.

At Waterloo the corps was commanded by General Olfermann and stood in reserve on the allied right for much of the battle. The light troops were engaged in Hougoumont Wood and the Brunswick infantry moved forward to stand in squares to protect the allied cannon during the massed French cavalry attacks. Some of the infantry battalions also joined the final advance and successfully cleared Hougoumont Wood at the end of the battle.

Some contemporary comments on the Brunswickers are less than complimentary, such as that of Captain Mercer of the Royal Horse Artillery, who describes them as 'mere boys' and claims that he constantly feared that they would flee if his artillerymen ran to take cover in their squares. But perhaps a fairer assessment is that of General Sir Henry Clinton, who wrote just before Waterloo that the Brunswick troops were of a very superior stature and excellent material for soldiers.

29 Officer's 1796 universal pattern gorget

THE GORGET WAS a last remnant of past ages when full body armour had been worn which included simple circular neck rings to protect the neck area. The throat – in French, *gorge* – was protected by the gorget.

Gradually over the centuries, the gorget became smaller and more symbolic, worn only as a status symbol linking its wearer to nobility and the age of chivalry, becoming a single crescent shape worn on a chain

Date of manufacture: c. 1796–1815

Location: Private collection

French gorget.

which became increasingly longer so that the gorget no longer protected the throat in normal wear.

The gorget was a small curved metal plate which was worn by officers to indicate their rank and that they were on duty. Gorgets were worn with a ribbon and rosette at each end, in the colour of the uniform facings of the regiment, excepting those who had facings of black, who were ordered to wear them with a red ribbon. The gorget was to be fastened to the top buttons of the jacket, and the lower part of it was not allowed to hang below the fifth button.

Gorgets ceased to be worn by British army officers in 1830, and by their French counterparts twenty years later. They were still worn to a limited extent in the Imperial German Army until 1914, as a special distinction for officers of the Prussian Gardes du Corps. Officers of the Spanish infantry continued to wear gorgets until the overthrow of the monarchy in 1931.

The gorget was revived as a uniform accessory during Germany's Third Reich, seeing widespread use within the German military and Nazi Party organisations.

30 Bayonet from a 'Brown Bess' musket

ALL INFANTRY MUSKETS and rifles were supplied with a bayonet of some fashion, to provide a close-quarter defence for an infantryman when the musket had been discharged. Alternatively, the bayonet could be used in offensive operations.

Bayonets originated alongside the development of firearms in the early seventeenth century, simply as a separate knife carried by musketeers as a defensive weapon of last resort. But by 1670 French infantry units were being issued with a 'plug bayonet' which fitted into the muzzle of the musket, giving the weapon a reach similar to that of the halberds carried by most infantry-men of the time. However, the plug bayonet prevented the musket being fired whilst in place and its use was soon abandoned. By the beginning of the eighteenth century, the 'socket bayonet' had been developed, which fitted onto the muzzle of the weapon and allowed firing and reloading to continue. This soon spread throughout Europe as the standard addition to a musket, although the design could vary from a small sword to a triangular pointed weapon.

By the time of the Napoleonic wars the bayonet was an essential part of the defence strategy for infantry

Date of manufacture:
c. 1810–15

Location:
Author's collection

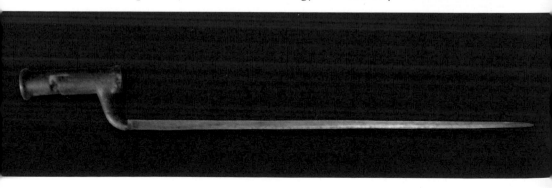

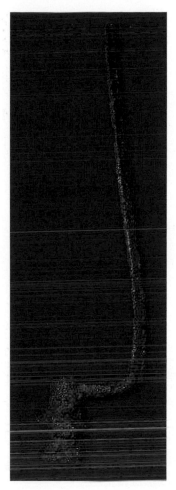

French bayonet discovered near Hougoumont.

threatened by cavalry. The infantry would draw up in a square formation four or more ranks deep, with the front ranks kneeling, protruding their muskets with bayonets attached out, rather like the spikes on a porcupine.

The bayonet could also be utilised in close combat, particularly when storming fortresses and clearing fortified defences, when halting the drive forward to reload would mean losing momentum. The bayonet was certainly used in action a great deal by both sides at the Battle of Ligny. At Plancenoit, where the constricted fighting meant that there was little opportunity to retire, the bayonet lent itself to hand-to-hand fighting.

The British, however, took its offensive use a step further; by utilising the bayonet's morale-sapping threat in close combat to break the stalemate of protracted firefights. It became standard practice for British battalions to deliver one or two crashing volleys of musketry, before giving a mighty 'Huzzah' and launching into an all-out bayonet charge.

It was found that few enemy soldiers would stand against a determined bayonet charge and traded bayonet thrusts. Indeed, instances of two protagonists both killing the other with a simultaneous bayonet thrust were so rare that it was always particularly noted when it did occur. In fact, it was more usual for one combatant or the other to turn tail to flee. Given the ascendancy that Wellington's troops had gained over the French in the Peninsular War, by Waterloo it was virtually a given that the French would not stand a determined bayonet charge by British troops, which gave the latter a greater advantage in terms of morale.

Surgeons of all armies rarely noted injuries by bayonet, but when they did the great majority are recorded as having been effected from behind – the wounded infantryman who lost his nerve and turned to flee was unable to retire quickly enough and was struck from behind,

We ought I have
more of the Cavalry
between the two
highs Roads. That is
Say three Brigades
at least besides the
Brigade in Strength
on the Right & having
the Belgian Cavalry

& the D. of Cumberland's
Hussars.

One heavy & one light
Brigade ought remain
on the Left.

31

Note by the Duke of Wellington

BATTLEFIELD COMMUNICATION WAS one of the greatest problems for commanders of this period, especially as the size of battlefields grew and it was now virtually impossible for commanders to see everything for themselves. They increasingly had to rely on corps commanders to follow instructions, and these instructions had to be communicated.

Pre-battle briefings were an obvious requirement and could be given in person, but other means were required to issue further orders when needed, as the situation on the battlefield changed, sometimes rapidly. Napoleon used a Chief of Staff, to whom he provided a generalised version of his plans. The Chief of Staff's role was to interpret these wishes and to issue specific orders to commanders to achieve the task. For the past fifteen years Marshal Louis Berthier had performed this role brilliantly, but when Napoleon returned from Elba, Berthier died, mysteriously falling from an upstairs window – whether suicide or murder has never been established. In Berthier's absence, Marshal Jean-de-Dieu Soult was given the role, one he was not overly familiar with and which he performed only adequately. The Prussian army ran a similar system, with Gneisenau serving as Chief of Staff to Marshal Blücher. These orders were produced and copied for all relevant commanders, and then

Date of production:
1815

Location:
Apsley House,
London, UK

aides-de-camp or cavalrymen provided as letter parties rode off with them at break-neck speed to find their intended recipient – not an easy task in the heat and smoke of battle. It was often necessary to send at least two copies of the message to its recipient by separate messengers to ensure its safe arrival, as many messengers were struck down en route. Indeed, there are many twists in the story of the Waterloo campaign, and many of these centre on the failure of orders to arrive or on significant delays in orders arriving.

Wellington, however, chose a more direct method, giving verbal orders directly to commanders or writing orders himself to speed up the system and also to ensure there was no misunderstanding. For this purpose he had requested the holsters on his saddle to be modified to allow him to carry writing implements. Using pads of goat skin, Wellington hastily pencilled his orders and despatched an aide to carry them to their recipient.

Amazingly, four of these notes still survive.

The first shown here was presumably sent to the Earl of Uxbridge and read:

> We ought to have more of the cavalry between the two high roads. That is to say three brigades at least besides the brigade in observation on the right, & besides the Belgian cavalry & the D. Of Cumberland's Hussars. One heavy & one light brigade might remain on the left.

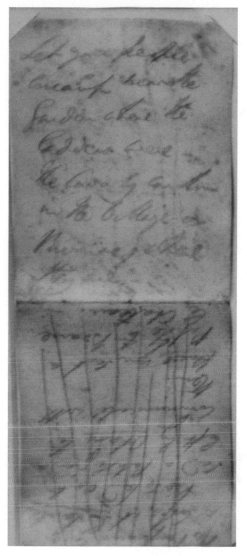

The second is perhaps the most famous, giving advice on defending the farm at Hougoumont while it was on fire. It reads:

I see that the fire has communicated from the haystack to the roof of the château. You must however still keep your men in those parts to which the fire does not reach. Take care that no men are lost by the falling in the roof, or floors. After they will have fallen in, occupy the ruined walls inside of the garden; particularly if it should be possible for the enemy to pass through the embers in the inside of the house.

A third exists, which actually has two messages on it. The first reads:

Let your people encamp near the garden where the ladders were. The cavalry canton in the village or bivouac where they are.

The second, which has been struck through, having presumably been despatched to Uxbridge previously, reads:

The Prussians have a corps at St Lambert. Be so kind as to send a patrole from our left by Ohain to communicate with them. Have you sent a patrol to Braine Le Chatcau[?]

32

Memorial cairn to the Duke of Richmond

CHARLES LENNOX, THE fourth Duke of Richmond (1764–1819), is probably best known as the husband of the duchess who gave the famous ball at Brussels on 15 June 1815. However, this is unfair, as he was a senior officer in the army and observed the battle as a civilian.

Lennox served in the Sussex militia for six years before joining the 7th Foot in 1785, and then as a captain in the 35th Foot. Within two years he had transferred as a captain to the Coldstream Guards, thanks to the influence of his uncle, the third Duke of Richmond.

Although he was a gregarious fellow and was loved by his troops, his seniors found him a difficult character with an apparent penchant for duelling. Soon after arriving in the Guards, he fought a duel with none other than the Duke of York, colonel of his regiment, when he actually fired and 'grazed His Royal Highness's curls' while York chose not to fire. He subsequently moved out of the Guards and returned to the 35th Foot as a lieutenant colonel. Within a couple of months he took part in another duel, this time against Theophilus Swift, regarding a pamphlet criticising Lennox's character; Swift was wounded but survived. That same year Lennox also married Lady Charlotte Gordon.

He became the fourth Duke of Richmond in 1806, on the death of his uncle. Despite his awkward relationship

Date of construction:
1819

Location:
Richmond, Ontario, Canada

with his seniors, he became Lord Lieutenant of Ireland in 1807, a post he retained until 1813, initially employing Arthur Wellesley (the future Duke of Wellington) as his secretary. By 1814 he was made a full general.

Richmond was a very keen cricketer, being an accomplished batsman and wicket keeper. He became a founder member of the Marylebone Cricket Club in 1786, when, together with the Earl of Winchilsea, he guaranteed Thomas Lord against any losses incurred in setting up a new cricket ground. This came to be known as Lord's Cricket Ground, the home of cricket.

In 1815 Richmond was living in Brussels, away from his many creditors, his excessive lifestyle having forced him to close the family home at Goodwood. It is often stated that the Duke of Richmond commanded the reserve in Wellington's army, but this is certainly incorrect: at the time he was officially governor of Plymouth, he was senior to the generals Wellington wished to employ in the army and he was not considered for any active role with the army in Belgium.

During the campaign, the Duke of Richmond rode to view the Battle of Waterloo, accompanied by his younger son, Lord William Pitt-Lennox, who was a cornet in the Blues and extra aide-de-camp to Major General Maitland. Pitt-Lennox was deemed unfit to serve in the battle because he was only 15 and had been severely wounded in a fall from his horse a few days previously, when he had broken his arm and lost his sight in one eye. Two older sons actually fought in the battle: Lieutenant Lord George Lennox, 9th Light Dragoons, as one of Wellington's aides-de-camp, and Captain The Earl of March, 52nd Foot as aide-de-camp to the Prince of Orange.

It is claimed that Wellington rebuked Richmond for his presence, saying, 'You have no business here,' but there is little evidence for this. Richmond remained at the scene of the battle, discussing movements with various officers, until he returned to Brussels with Pitt-Lennox shortly after the heavy cavalry charged d'Erlon's corps. At Paris, soon after the battle, the duke was horrified to hear that his daughter, Lady Sarah Lennox, had

eloped with General Maitland, but eventually accepted the marriage.

Returning to their life in Brussels, he was surprised by an offer of appointment as Governor General of British North America (Canada), which he accepted immediately and arrived there with his family in July 1818. In the summer of 1819, he began a tour of Canada but was bitten by a fox and died in agony of rabies at the Masonic Arms tavern, in Richmond, a settlement already named after the new governor. His body was transported to Quebec and he was buried there in Holy Trinity Cathedral.

33

Belgic shako

THE WEARING OF headgear by the infantry was originally instigated to provide some protection from rain, and if the headgear had a visor it would protect the wearer from the sun. It also offered some very limited protection from sword blows.

Taller hats and helmets were also intended to make the men appear taller, and thus, it was hoped, unnerve their enemies by their physical stature. It is very doubtful, however, whether this had any real effect. The differing shapes of the headgear of the armies did help to identify troops at a distance when their bright uniforms were so worn and patched on campaign that the original colour was difficult to ascertain or when plain greatcoats worn over the jacket obscured the colour.

During the Napoleonic wars the traditional two-pointed hat, the bicorn, had been phased out by all armies by about 1812 and replaced by cylindrical hats with peaks, commonly known as shakos. Much of the British army then sported a round flat-topped hat known as a 'stovepipe' because of its similarity in look to the black pipe that funnelled off the smoke from stoves. By the time of Waterloo the infantry had replaced this with the 'Belgic' shako, issued for the Belgian campaign, which sported a high front peak to reinforce the illusion of height. This shako was also issued in huge

Date of manufacture: c. 1815

Location: Private collection

Lieutenant John Bramwell's 92nd Foot stovepipe cap.

numbers by the British government to the newly raised units of the Netherlands army, and many Belgian units wore them at Waterloo.

The French shako was wider at the top and narrowed towards the head. This shape of hat was quite prevalent at the battle on both sides; the Nassau troops who had recently fought with the French retained this kind of shako. The light dragoon regiments had been refitted with similar shakos, and the Prince Regent also favoured this style of cap.

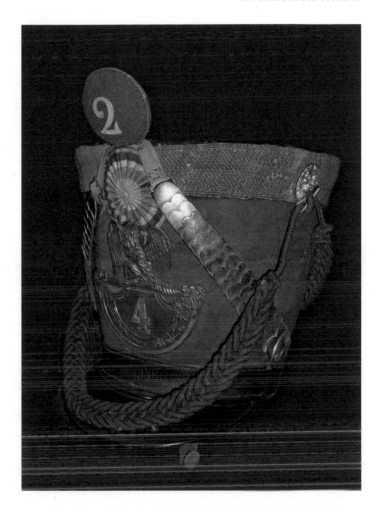

French shako of the 2nd Battalion of the 4ème Régiment de Ligne.

Such prevalence of this French-style shako did lead to unfortunate 'friendly fire' situations between allied forces, with Prussian infantry opening fire on the Nassau troops defending Papelotte, having mistaken them for Frenchmen. It is also almost certain that both Prussian and British infantry did at times mistakenly shoot at British light dragoons during the confusion of the final rout of the French army, because of their use of this shape of shako.

The Prince Regent did not learn from these awkward occurrences and within a few years of Waterloo the entire British army were wearing bell tops, but luckily they did not go to war with the French again.

34 Baker rifle

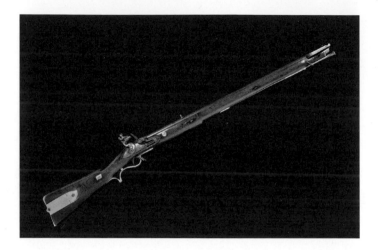

FOR MOST OF the infantry at the Battle of Waterloo, the main weapon was a musket of some design. These muskets were all smooth-bore weapons, which meant that the lead ball fitted only loosely and was fired out of the barrel without imparting any spin, which caused the musket to be very inaccurate beyond 50 yards or so.

Rifles were considered inferior by many, largely because the tactics of the day called for rapid fire at a large mass of men at close range – something that required only the most basic instruction. A rifle, on the other hand, was capable of being used for aimed shots to target individuals at over twice the range of a musket, but was much slower to load, since the ball had to fit tightly in the bore, and it required a good level of marksmanship to master. Most military powers, including Napoleon's French army, decided that the cost of the guns and the training required was just not worth it.

It had already been discovered as early as the 1750s that adding rifling to the inside of the barrel produced a spin to a tight-fitting ball which helped to increase accuracy dramatically, and a number of German states experimented with such early rifled weapons. The

Date of manufacture:
c. 1813

Location:
Private collection

British army had learned the value of rifled weapons from its painful experience of facing the American revolutionaries. However, existing rifle designs were considered too cumbersome, slow-firing, fragile and expensive to be used on any scale beyond irregular companies.

It was not until 1800 that the British army produced a standard-issue British-made rifle for some of its forces. Before the Experimental Rifle Corps was formed, the British Board of Ordnance held a trial at Woolwich Arsenal to select a standard rifle pattern; the rifle chosen was designed by master gunsmith Ezekiel Baker.

The final model accepted had a barrel 30in long, and the ball used was the same size as that used in the short-barrelled cavalry musket known as a carbine, with a mere quarter-turn in the barrel to give it spin. The stocks were made of walnut and had a metal locking bar to accommodate a fearsome 24in sword bayonet. As gunpowder fouled the barrel with use, the weapon became much slower to load and less accurate, so a cleaning kit was stored in a small compartment in the rifle butt. This was to become known colloquially as the Baker rifle, after its inventor, although it was always officially known as the pattern 1800 infantry rifle.

The Baker was reported to be effective at long range due to its accuracy and dependability under battlefield conditions, but was issued officially only to rifle regiments, particularly the famous 95th Foot, which had parts of all three battalions at Waterloo. A few other regiments, such as the 23rd Royal Welch Fusiliers, acquired rifles for its light companies. The two light infantry battalions of the King's German Legion as well as sharpshooter platoons within the light companies of the legion's line battalions also used the Baker rifle at Waterloo.

The Baker rifle could not usually be reloaded as fast as a musket, as the slightly undersized lead balls had to be wrapped in patches of greased leather or linen so that they would fit more closely in the rifling. A rifleman was expected to be able to fire two aimed shots a minute, compared to the four shots a minute by the Brown Bess musket in the hands of a trained infantryman.

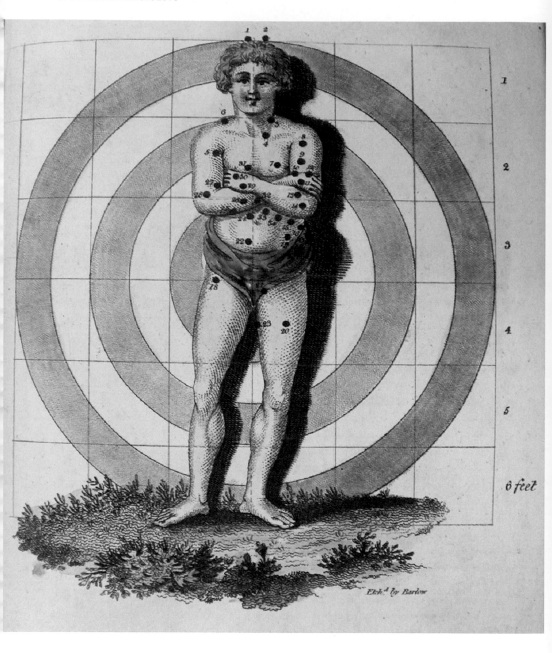

Image of target used
by Ezekiel Baker,
showing results of
thirty-four shot at 100
yards from a Baker
rifle.

The rifle was capable of accurate firing at a range of up to 200 yards (183m), whereas the musket was only accurate up to about 100 yards (91m). In fact, standing at 100 yards from a musket-armed opponent you would be very unlikely to be struck by an aimed shot, but with a rifle-armed opponent, you were almost certain to be struck.

The tactics of infantry armed with rifles were markedly different to those of their musket-armed counterparts. Because of the slower rate of fire, but greater accuracy, they were used in a more independent role, usually skirmishing in front of the main line in pairs, utilising cover to protect themselves. Their aim was to disrupt the command and control structure of the enemy force by targeting officers, NCOs and drummers. However, at Waterloo Wellington used many of the rifle-armed units as line infantry in tight formation – an unusual tactic.

Troops issued with the Baker rifle were also required to serve as regular infantry if required. The higher rate of fire (and therefore, volume of fire) of the musket was required when deployed as line infantry, even if it came with a loss of accuracy. For this reason, ammunition was issued in two forms to the riflemen: greased patches for accurate shooting, and paper cartridges with reduced diameter balls that would slide easily down even a fouled bore for rapid fire.

35 Musket balls

MUSKETS WERE THE main armament used on the battlefield of Waterloo and during the nine hours of the battle it is estimated that over 3.5 million musket or pistol balls were fired, which caused fewer than 20,000 casualties.

Musket balls were made of lead, which, being malleable, could be moulded easily into round balls with hand tools. They varied in size from the larger Prussian balls (19.5 mm diameter), through the British to the smaller French balls (17.2mm diameter), with pistol balls being smaller again. Lead balls do not erode much in soil, and thousands are collected from the battlefield every year, many almost as perfect as the day they were fired.

It has been shown that musket balls fired at close range could penetrate wood or even the iron cuirasses, but at greater distance they were literally flattened on

Date of manufacture: 1815

Location: Private collection

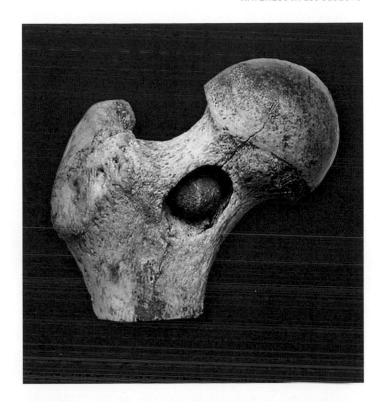

Head of a femur with a musket ball injury which has unusually remained spherical without flattening.

striking a solid surface and failed to penetrate. Indeed, there are many recorded instances of soldiers being struck by a ball close to the end of its flight, when it contained little kinetic energy. These were known as 'spent' balls and failed to penetrate the skin but caused severe bruising and winded the victim, leaving many to believe at first that they had been severely wounded.

Balls that struck with full force had a devastating effect on the body, often dragging dirty particles of clothing into the wound which caused sepsis and tearing through muscle and vital organs on their passage. Many balls failed to pass entirely through the body and required removal by surgery. Often they proved impossible to extract and were carried deep within the wound, but frequently worked themselves towards the surface over many years and were eventually removed by simply excising the skin.

If the ball struck bone it would flatten on impact and often shatter the bone, leaving little hope of the bone recovering and requiring amputation.

36 Hussar uniform
of Colonel Marbot of the 7th Hussars

COLONEL JEAN BAPTISTE, Baron de Marbot, was an extremely experienced and able light cavalry officer who had fought in Napoleon's army for many years, serving at the battles of Austerlitz, Jena, Friedland, Aspern-Essling and Borodino before being present at Waterloo. He wrote a very lively set of memoirs about his military life, almost certainly exaggerated, but which Sir Arthur Conan Doyle used as a model for his novels about Brigadier Gerard. However, he ended his memoirs with the campaign of 1814 and avoided writing much about the Waterloo campaign; what he did record about it is contradictory.

However, he was stationed on the far right of the French line and was one of the first to encounter the Prussians, therefore his evidence is important and vital to our understanding of this sector of the battlefield. He apparently wrote a report on the battle for Marshal Davout in 1815; there is no copy of this still in existence, but on 26 June 1815 he did write a letter in which he simply stated that he commanded his hussars and a battalion of infantry and two cannon on the right flank, although he does not give precise details.

He was positioned there to look out for the arrival of Marshal Grouchy's corps but was surprised by the sudden arrival of Blücher's Prussians. Outflanked and overwhelmed, at some point he received a wound from a Prussian lance. Captain Dupuy, who commanded a squadron in the 7th Hussars, records that they stood on the edge of the battle as 'mere spectators' until after 4 p.m., when they were suddenly attacked by Prussian uhlans, during which Marbot was wounded by a lance.

Fifteen years later, in a letter written to Marshal Grouchy, Marbot relates how he was initially stationed with his regiment and a battalion of infantry

Date of manufacture:
1812–15

Location:
Musée de l'Armée,
Paris, France

near Frichermont, where he soon received orders to search beyond St Lambert for signs of Grouchy. He claims that one of his patrols discovered the Prussians near St Lambert, capturing a Prussian officer and some men, who were immediately sent on to Napoleon. He was soon forced back, but sent numerous reports to his emperor of the Prussian advance, which were apparently always answered with the reply that they were definitely Grouchy's troops. This second report, written many years later, was clearly an attempt to make his report match that of Napoleon's regarding his knowledge of the Prussian flank march. It can be discounted, particularly as Marbot had also been a beneficiary of Napoleon's will.

More recently it has become clear that it cannot be true that Napoleon had seen the Prussians at St Lambert at 1 p.m. and had it confirmed by a captured Prussian (see item 65), allowing him sufficient time to have Soult place an addendum to the orders to Grouchy. Indeed, there is now much doubt regarding the legitimacy of this order, which does not appear in the imperial correspondence logs and only emerged a few years after the battle. The Prussian appearance on the battlefield was almost certainly a complete shock to Napoleon's troops.

37 Farm of Mont St Jean

THE FARM OF Mont St Jean stands alongside the main Brussels highway, 1 mile north of the allied front line at the Battle of Waterloo. Further north, the straggling village of Mont St Jean stretched alongside the road, numbering only a dozen houses or so. Even to this day many French people refer to the 'Battle of Mont St Jean' rather than Waterloo, which in terms of locality is actually more accurate.

The family who owned the property were thought to have abandoned the farm and fled, but it seems that the wife of the farmer hid in the attic, hoping to help save her livestock from marauding soldiers. Here she apparently sat out the entire battle, seeing nothing and hearing little above the general noise of battle, except

Date of construction: 1719

Location: Waterloo, Belgium

the terrible cries of the wounded as they went under the knife. It is unlikely that she saved any of her livestock.

The situation of the farm made it an obvious location for an advanced field hospital. With little time to prepare the site and no such thing as sterile surgical facilities, kitchen and dining tables served as makeshift operating tables, and even doors were taken down and placed across two barrels for the same use. With clean straw for the wounded to lie on and buckets to receive the discarded limbs, the building was ready.

No sooner had the battle commenced than the stream of men bearing horrific wounds began to pour in at a great rate. Wounds were quickly assessed, but there was no triage: it was simply a case of first come, first served, although seniority did help. Those with no hope of survival were simply laid out in the barns to die, others with minor wounds regarded as 'recoverable' were dressed and laid alongside the dying, often after enduring the surgeon prodding deep into the wounds to remove the lead balls and fragments of clothing which had been driven deep into them. Those with terrible wounds to limbs were soon selected for amputation.

So many operations were carried out that day that eyewitnesses record seeing huge heaps of discarded limbs simply piled up in the courtyard as they were discarded from the operating rooms. It was not long before the farm was full of wounded, and evidence appears to indicate that cartloads of men were then ferried on to Brussels, to allow more to be treated; indeed the surgeons apparently did not stop amputating limbs all night.

The threat of a French victory failed to prevent the surgeons from continuing their work, nor did the frequent cannonballs from ricocheting shots striking the walls deter them, although there are reports that some of the wounded fled to Brussels during the frequent alarms that the French were coming.

The farm has recently been repaired and it would make the perfect site for a museum to the medical services in the battle; it is hoped that this will come to fruition in the future.

38 Highland infantry officer's sword

THERE WERE THREE battalions of Highlanders at Waterloo, wearing the bonnet and kilt as their uniform: the 42nd (Royal Highlanders, who became the Black Watch), the 79th (Cameron Highlanders) and the 92nd (Gordon Highlanders), these were all in Picton's Division, but were not in the same brigade together. The kilt was a new sight for both the Belgian civilians, who found them very friendly and gentle guests, and the French troops, who discovered they were savage in battle. These regiments were based around the clan system with many men coming from the estates of their colonels. The Highland officers carried a wide sword with an ornate guard, a modern descendant of the traditional Highland broadsword.

These Highland troops were heavily engaged at the Battle of Quatre Bras, where the 42nd was caught by French lancers before they had successfully formed

Date of manufacture:
c. 1815

Location:
Private collection

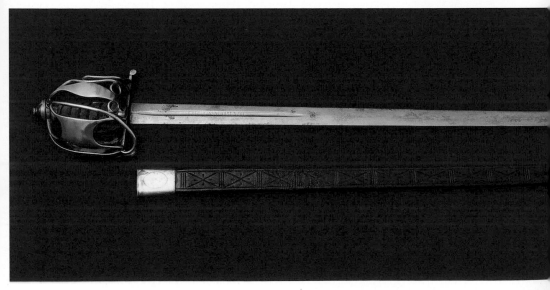

A French cartoon of Highlanders in Paris.

square. The lancers penetrated and could have destroyed the battalion, but it completed the formation and killed all of the French cavalrymen who were trapped inside, at a significant loss to the Highlanders. The 92nd was later ordered to retake the house and gardens known as La Bergerie, but suffered severely in hand-to-hand fighting to clear the property. Two of the battalions lost their commanders during the battle; the wounded Lieutenant Colonel Sir Robert Macara of the 42nd was killed by French cavalry whilst being escorted from the field on a blanket stretcher.

At Waterloo, these regiments were involved in the repulse of the Comte d'Erlon's attack against Wellington's left at around 1.30 p.m. Although they fought bravely, it is probable that they would have been overwhelmed by numbers, but they were saved by the appearance of the British heavy cavalry, which decimated the French infantry.

Stories of soldiers of the 92nd holding the stirrups of the Scots Greys to charge with them are almost certainly fanciful.

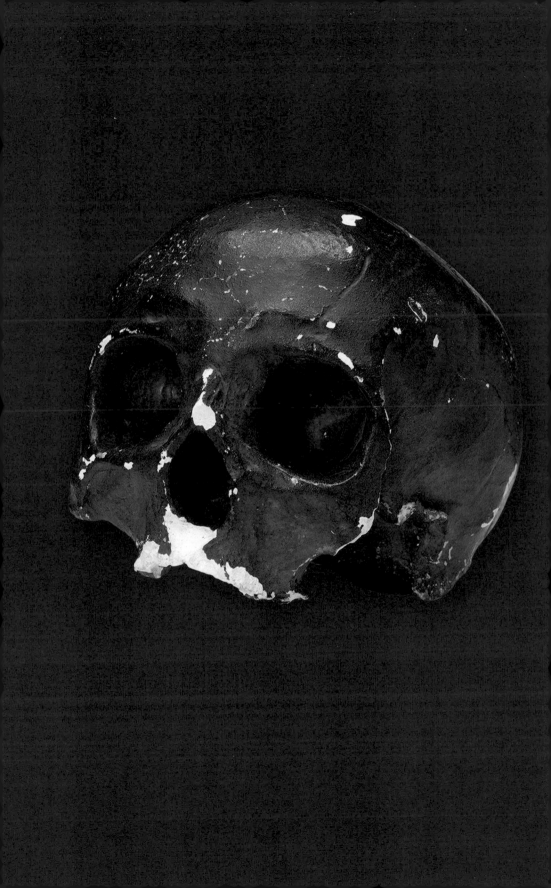

39

Cast of the skull of Corporal John Shaw

THE MOST FAMOUS soldier in the British army was undoubtedly Corporal of Horse (equal to a Sergeant) John Shaw of the 2nd Life Guards, who was killed at Waterloo. Indeed, Charles Dickens wrote in *Bleak House* that Shaw was 'The model of the whole British Army'.

John Shaw was born in 1789, the son of a farmer in Wollaton, Nottinghamshire. His strength as a boxer was apparent even at school, but in 1807, at the age of 18, Shaw joined the Life Guards. Here his officers quickly learned of his boxing abilities and he was soon boxing in matches against professionals at Jackson's Rooms at 13 Bond Street in London. In 1812 he was persuaded to enter the prize ring and won his bout. His renown was so great that in early 1815 he offered to fight any man in England. He defeated Henry Painter in April, but before he could meet Tom Cribb, the champion boxer, he was called to serve in the Waterloo campaign.

At just over 6ft tall and solidly built, he was often used as a model by Haydon the sculptor. As well as having a reputation for his boxing, he was also renowned as an expert swordsman.

Despite premonitions of death, Shaw rode into battle on 18 June 1815 without fear. He was killed. Perhaps unsurprisingly, given the confusion of the cavalry melee, the circumstances of his death are obscure.

Date of construction:
1815

Location:
Life Guards Museum, London, UK

1796 pattern heavy cavalry sword.

Some claim that he was shot, others state that, having defeated a number of cuirassiers who surrounded him, he eventually succumbed to numerous wounds and had the coup de grace administered to him by a mere drummer boy (this is claimed by Victor Hugo, in perhaps a play on the David and Goliath story).

Nobody will ever be sure of his exploits that day, but given his prodigious strength of body and will power, it seems hard to believe that Shaw would sell his life short. Stories of his cleaving the helmeted heads of cuirassiers clean in two may or may not be true, but the most believable version is that written by his friend Private Thomas Playford:

> On the following morning we went in search of the surviving fragments of our regiment, and found a few officers and men; perhaps twenty in all including ourselves. In this search I rode across one part of the field of battle, and Corporal Webster pointed out to me the dead body of Shaw, pointing to a spot where several dead French soldiers lay, said 'There lies Shaw'. I replied 'I rode over that ground this

morning, and noticed that one of our regiment was among the slain, but his face was concealed'. Webster said 'I examined the countenance and recognised Shaw. He appears to have received a fatal injury in his body, for there is a deep wound in his side, near the heart, which appears to have been inflicted with either a bayonet or a lance' ... As I did not witness the exploits of Shaw in close combat, nor yet inquire of the wounded French soldiers near his corpse, by whose hand the dead lying roundabout had fallen, I can neither add to, nor take away from the published accounts; but from the position in which Shaw's remains were found among dead adversaries, with only one or two killed Englishmen near, this seems to favour what has been said concerning the havoc he produced among the French troopers before he fell. What I knew of him would favour this: for he was the strongest and most resolute man I ever knew, and had such great confidence in his own prowess that he would not hesitate to attack as many foes as could stand opposed to him

Shaw was buried in a mass grave on the battlefield, but it would appear that his head was removed and returned to Britain. Sir Walter Scott, who was enthralled by the battle, arranged to have a plaster cast made of the skull. The whereabouts of the skull are no longer known.

40 Hougoumont crucifix

ONE OF THE most extraordinary and iconic images of Waterloo is that of the oak crucifix that escaped the flames as the farm at Hougoumont was burned to the ground during the fighting. Château d'Hougoumont stood in the centre of the farmstead and was set on fire, probably by French incendiary shells, in the middle of the afternoon (see item 22).

The soldiers of the Coldstream Guards stationed in the upper rooms of the château, where they could fire over the walls, were forced to remain at their posts until the very last moment. Private Mathew Clay recalls that his company officer stood at the top of the stairs with drawn sword, to prevent them leaving. Eventually, however, the fire became so fierce that they were forced to abandon their posts and, although they did manage to escape, few emerged from the château without scorch marks. The fire engulfed the entire property and the roof of the château collapsed inwards, leaving a few stone walls standing amongst the smouldering ruins.

However, in what seemed a miracle, the small chapel attached to the château, where the huge fifteenth-century wooden carving of Jesus on the Cross, measuring 6ft 6in (2m) high and 6ft 6in (2m) wide, hung on the wall, escaped virtually untouched. The only evidence of the fierceness of the fire was the scorched feet of Christ. It seems that at this point the fire receded and burned itself out.

Victor Hugo described the crucifix in his novel, *Les Misérables:*

The flames filled this building; it was a perfect furnace; the door was burned, the floor was burned, the wooden Christ was not burned. The fire preyed

Date of construction:
Sixteenth century

Location:
Presently unknown

upon his feet, of which only the blackened stumps are now to be seen; then it stopped, – a miracle, according to the assertion of the people of the neighbourhood.

The chapel and crucifix became a shrine for visitors to Hougoumont.

Unfortunately, in 2011, when the farm was no longer lived in, thieves broke into the chapel even though it was alarmed; they dismantled stonework around the door and removed the bolt. They then restored the lock and masonry, disguising the theft for several days. It would seem that the crucifix was stolen to order, for a private collector, but during the process of removal several large splinters of wood were broken off the figure of Christ itself.

Belgian police alerted Interpol in case an attempt was made to smuggle the huge cross, which weighs 31st (200kg), to another country. As this book goes to print, it has been announced that the battered remains of the crucifix have been recovered and it is hoped that it will be restored and replaced to its rightful home.

41

Remains of a Congreve rocket

PERHAPS THE MOST unusual weapon used at Waterloo was the Congreve rocket, fired either lying down on the ground at approaching troops, or with a high trajectory from a large tripod or bombarding frame.

The British experienced the use of rockets for the first time during their wars with the various Indian armies they encountered as they took control of that country. It was reported that at the siege of Seringapatam the British army had suffered more from the rockets than from the shells or any other weapon used by the enemy. This led the Royal Arsenal to begin its own set of trials in 1801. The development work was chiefly done by William Congreve who set up a research and development programme at the arsenal's laboratory. He was the son of Lieutenant General Sir William Congreve, the comptroller of the Royal Laboratories at the Royal Arsenal.

The rocket was made up of an iron case containing black powder for propulsion and a conical warhead. The rockets were attached to wooden guide poles and were launched from half-troughs on simple metal A-frames. They could be fired up to two miles, the range being set by the degree of elevation of the launching frame, although at any range they were fairly inaccurate and had a tendency for premature explosion. They were as much a psychological weapon as a physical one, and

Congreve rocket on a bombarding frame.

Date of manufacture: c. 1814

Location: Private collection

they were rarely or never used except alongside other types of artillery. Congreve designed several different warhead sizes, from 3 to 24lb (1.4 to 10.9kg). The 24lb type with a 15ft (4.6m) guide pole was the most widely used variant. Different warheads were used, including explosive, shrapnel (designed to explode at head height) and incendiary. The rockets were launched using a flintlock mechanism, triggered by pulling a long cord. They were manufactured at a special facility near the Waltham Abbey Royal Gunpowder Mills beside the river Lea in Essex.

The Royal Navy used rockets quite enthusiastically as part of the huge payload crammed into fire ships, designed to cause consternation and panic in enemy shipping. The flammability of rockets meant they were deemed impractical and downright dangerous for any other use on the wooden warships until late in the wars.

In 1807 during the bombardment of Copenhagen about 300 Congreve rockets were fired and in 1813 Danzig was similarly attacked, setting the city's food stores on fire and resulting in its surrender. The British army converted two troops of Royal Horse Artillery to carry rockets. The only British unit at the 'Battle of the Nations' at Leipzig in October 1813 was a detachment of Royal Horse Artillery armed with Congreve rockets.

Rockets seem to have been used more frequently during the war with the United States over Canada, generally known as the War of 1812. It was the use of ship-launched Congreve rockets by the British in the bombardment of Fort McHenry in the US in 1814 that inspired the fifth line of 'The Star-Spangled Banner': 'And the rockets' red glare, the bombs bursting in air'.

At Waterloo one troop of Royal Horse Artillery, commanded by Captain Edward Whinyates, carried rockets, but was also ordered to man a full complement of six cannon as the Duke of Wellington had little confidence in the rockets. Although there are a few examples of a rocket causing massive devastation, there are hundreds more that describe wayward rockets which hissed across the countryside in all directions, with a few even turning on their launchers.

The rockets were, however, used effectually on the retreat to Waterloo, reportedly scoring a direct hit on a French battery it opposed. It is also known that when d'Erlon's corps was defeated at Waterloo by the British heavy cavalry, a squad of rocketeers proceeded into the valley and fired a large number of rockets along the ground after the fleeing French. There are few reports of specific losses, but many of the French cavalry describe the confusion such a screeching, flaming weapon caused, snaking towards the massed cavalry ranks.

Although a civilian, Congreve was awarded the honorary rank of lieutenant colonel in the Hanoverian army's artillery in 1811 and is often referred to as 'Colonel Congreve'. Later he was made major general in the same army. He was awarded the Order of St George of Russia following the Battle of Leipzig in 1813 and in 1816 he was made Knight Commander of the Royal Guelphic Order of Hanover. In 1821 he was awarded the Order of the Sword by the King of Sweden.

After a major fraud case began against him in 1826 he fled to France, where he was taken seriously ill. He was prosecuted in his absence, with the Lord Chancellor ultimately ruling, just before Congreve's death, that the transaction was 'clearly fraudulent' and designed to profit Congreve and others.

He died in Toulouse, France in May 1828, aged 55.

42 La Haye Sainte Farm

LA HAYE SAINTE Farm (the name translates as 'the sacred hedge') is a walled farmhouse at the foot of the allied ridge on the main Charleroi to Brussels road. As such it formed an ad hoc bastion in front of the allied centre, making it imperative that the French capture it before they could break through Wellington's lines.

During the night of 17 June 1815, the main door into the great barn of the farm was used as firewood by occupying allied troops. However, they then obstructed the doorway as best they could with farm implements, the gates were all barricaded, firing steps were prepared and loopholes dug out of the walls with their bayonets to fire through. An obstruction (or abatis) was also placed on the *chaussée*, made of farm machinery, timber and any other materials to hand.

The troops destined to defend the farm complex were the 2nd Light Battalion King's German Legion commanded by Major Georg Baring, numbering about 400 men, and part of the 1st Light Battalion King's German

Date of construction:
c. 1700

Location:
Waterloo battlefield, Belgium

Legion. During the battle, they were further supported by around 200 Nassau troops and the light company of the 5th Line Battalion of the King's German Legion. Unfortunately, no further reserve of rifle ammunition was supplied before the action commenced; as it was so far in advance of the main line, resupply proved incredibly difficult once the action had begun.

The first attack against La Haye Sainte was made around 2 p.m. during d'Erlon's massive assault against Wellington's left wing. The attack failed and the French received heavy losses, fired on from the walls, through the door panels and from the loopholes – almost every shot struck home. It was not uncommon for a rifle ball to pass through two or three bodies in the dense crowd that surged up to the gates.

Several further attempts to take the farm failed until, around 6 p.m., the defenders ran short of ammunition and were eventually forced to abandon the post, retiring through the farmhouse to the relative safety of the allied ridge behind. When the French eventually broke in, a number of the defenders were killed in ferocious hand-to-hand combat, but there was no massacre as some report – many were taken prisoner and escorted to the rear. It is often erroneously claimed that of the farm's 870 defenders only forty-three survived. However, this claim arises from a misinterpretation of Major Baring's report: in fact, around 550 of the garrison reported for duty the following day, uninjured.

The capture of the farm allowed the French to bring up their cannon to fire from its cover, and to assert a great deal of pressure on the allied centre. However, riflemen of the 95th Foot were able to pick off some of the gunners, so the cannon were largely ineffective.

When the Imperial Guard attacked in the final phase of the battle, they were supported by the French troops around La Haye Sainte, but during their subsequent retreat the farm was abandoned and the allies recaptured it, seemingly without a struggle.

Today La Haye Sainte is privately owned as a working farm and family home, and unfortunately – although understandably – visitors are unwelcome.

43 Jacket of Surgeon Larrey

DOMINIQUE JEAN LARREY (1766–1842) was a noted French surgeon and an important innovator in battlefield medicine, and this is one of his jackets worn when on campaign.

Larrey was born in the Pyrenees. He was orphaned at the age of 13 and was then raised by his uncle Alexis, who was chief surgeon in Toulouse. After serving a ten-year apprenticeship, he went to Paris to study, but his studies were cut short by war.

He specialised in surgery and initially served in the French navy; he became chief surgeon to the frigate *Vigilante* on its voyage to North America but had to resign from the navy due to chronic seasickness. In 1789 he was called up for military service to defend the new Republic.

Larrey was not comfortable with the traditional role of an army surgeon: he did not wait until the casualties were brought to him at the rear of the field but flung himself into the fray to help them. He accompanied Napoleon on his expeditions to Egypt, and in 1805 was appointed surgeon-in-chief to the French army. He followed Napoleon throughout his campaigns across Europe and in the disastrous march on Moscow. Larrey was a favourite of Napoleon, who commented, 'If the army ever erects a monument to express its gratitude, it should do so in honour of Larrey.' He was made a baron at the Battle of Wagram in 1809.

Date of manufacture:
c. 1815

Location:
Private collection

Replica of Larrey's ambulance.

During this time, Larrey initiated the modern method of army surgery with improved organisation of field hospitals, and he began the first army ambulance corps. Larrey adapted his ambulances for the rapid transport of the wounded and manned them with trained crews of drivers, litter bearers and medical staff consisting of a doctor, two assistants and a nurse. This medical team provided first aid and had a carriage to evacuate the casualties. This method, which was revolutionary at that time, saved many soldiers who would previously have suffered for hours, sometimes days on end, without receiving any medical attention.

Larrey established a rule for the triage of casualties, treating the wounded according to the seriousness of their injuries and urgency of need for medical care, regardless of their rank or nationality. He was one of the first to describe the therapeutic use of maggots and performed one of the first amputations at the hip and of the shoulder joint.

At Waterloo his courage under fire was reputedly noticed by the Duke of Wellington, who ordered his artillery not to fire in his direction so as to 'give the brave man time to gather up the wounded' but this is probably a myth as it would be very difficult to make out any individual during such chaos and in such a smoke-filled atmosphere.

At the Battle of Waterloo, Larrey was taken prisoner by the Prussians, who wanted to execute him. However, he was recognised by one of the German surgeons, who pleaded for his life. Marshal Blücher remembered that Larrey had saved the life of his son a few years earlier, and so Larrey was spared and was invited to Blücher's dinner table as a guest and taken back to France under escort. He devoted the remainder of his life to writing and a civilian medical career until his death on 25 July 1842 in Lyon.

44 Nassau Waterloo medal

THE NASSAU MEDAL was instituted in December 1815 for all Nassau troops present in the Waterloo campaign. It bears the portrait of Duke Frederick August and a winged Victory on the reverse.

The German duchies of Nassau-Usingen and Nassau-Weilburg had joined the Confederation of the Rhine in 1806, formed by Napoleon to supersede the ancient Holy Roman Empire, which had been controlled by the Habsburgs of Austria.

The Nassau troops had originally fought with Napoleon's armies, but when the duchy was freed of French troops in 1813 they changed sides. The French were aware of the situation and some Nassau units were forced to lay down their weapons, but others managed

Date of manufacture: 1815

Location: Private collection

LA BELLE ALLIANCE

Nassau troops at the
Battle of Waterloo.

to elude them and marched to join Wellington's army. Three Nassau regiments fought at Waterloo. Two were part of the Netherlands army – the Orange-Nassau Regiment, which ranked as no. 28 in the Netherlands line – and the 2nd Nassau-Usingen Light Infantry. The third regiment present was the 1st Nassau Regiment, which remained a separate Nassau contingent.

These troops played a significant role in holding the crossroads at Quatre Bras on the evening of 15 June and morning of 16 June against Marshal Ney's advance guard. At Waterloo a battalion of the 2nd Regiment, commanded by Major Busgen, played a major part in the defence of Hougoumont, and later 200 men of this battalion went into La Haye Sainte to aid the defence of that farmstead. The majority of the rest of the Netherlands Nassau contingent were posted in the hamlets of La Haye, Frichermont and Papelotte, where they skirmished all day with Durutte's division. The 1st Nassau Regiment was involved in repelling the massed cavalry attacks, but was severely battered as these inexperienced troops could apparently only form a solid column, which was very susceptible to artillery fire.

Near the end of the battle, elements of the Prussian army arrived in the area near Papelotte and mistook the Nassau troops in their French-style uniforms for French troops, and a number were hit by 'friendly fire'. Thankfully the mistake was soon rectified and no serious harm done.

When the ruling head of Nassau-Usingen, Frederick August, died in March 1816, the whole of Nassau was unified under Frederick William of Nassau-Weilburg, as Duke of Nassau: the united state passing to his son William, who succeeded him in the same year.

45

Coatee of a soldier of the King's German Legion

WHEN IN 1803 the Electorate of Hanover, which still remained within the control of George III of Great Britain, was overrun by French forces, Germans loyal to the Crown fled to Britain in such numbers that a unit of infantry was ordered to be raised, to be known as the King's German Regiment. Such numbers of all three arms of the military service arrived that this quickly mushroomed into the King's German Legion (KGL) of around 14,000 men.

The legion included five regiments of cavalry, ten battalions of infantry – two light and eight line – and six batteries of artillery with a company of engineers. A number of units fought during the Peninsular War, gaining a reputation for both professionalism and bravery, and were regarded as equal to the best battalions in the British army. The cavalry were regarded as the best in the army and were renowned for the care they took of their horses.

Date of manufacture:
c. 1815

Location:
King's German Legion Museum, Celle, Germany

When the war ended in 1814, the legion came together in Belgium, where it was intended that they would disband and be assimilated within the army of the newly proclaimed Kingdom of Hanover. Uncertainty about their future and perhaps a feeling that their services had been forgotten by the British establishment led to a severe drop in the troops' morale at this point. However,

149

Hanoverian Waterloo medal.

fortuitously for Britain, the battalions had not yet been disbanded when Napoleon reappeared and, when asked to extend their term of service for another six months, they agreed almost to a man. Dressed in British red coats, these troops looked and acted as British infantry to their French opponents, although their orders of command were made in German.

However, the numbers of men in each battalion had dwindled to around 500 men each because of retirement or incapacity, which meant that there was a surplus of officers and NCOs. On 25 April 1815 an order was sent out that each King's German Legion battalion would reduce from ten to six companies and the spare officers and NCOs were transferred to the newly raised Hanoverian levies to bolster their command structures.

At Waterloo, the 1st Brigade KGL under Colonel du Plat, consisting of line battalions 1 to 4, remained in reserve until the middle of the afternoon and then stood behind the covered way on the edge of Hougoumont orchard and supported those troops who were trying to maintain it against strong French opposition.

The 2nd Brigade KGL, under the command of Colonel Ompteda, consisting of the two light battalions and the 5th and 8th line battalions, stood near La Haye Sainte. The 2nd Light Battalion, commanded by Major Baring, was the primary force utilised in the defence of this farm (see item 42). However, both the 5th and 8th battalions suffered heavily on separate occasions, caught in line by French cuirassiers when trying to support those within La Haye Sainte.

The legion cavalry fought bravely, particularly in counter-attacks against the French cavalry charges, but did not play any key role. The artillery too performed with great professionalism throughout.

At the end of 1815 the King's German Legion marched from occupied France to Hanover, where it eventually disbanded and the men either retired or were assimilated into the Hanoverian army. The Hanoverian troops both received the Hanoverian Waterloo medal and the British Waterloo medal.

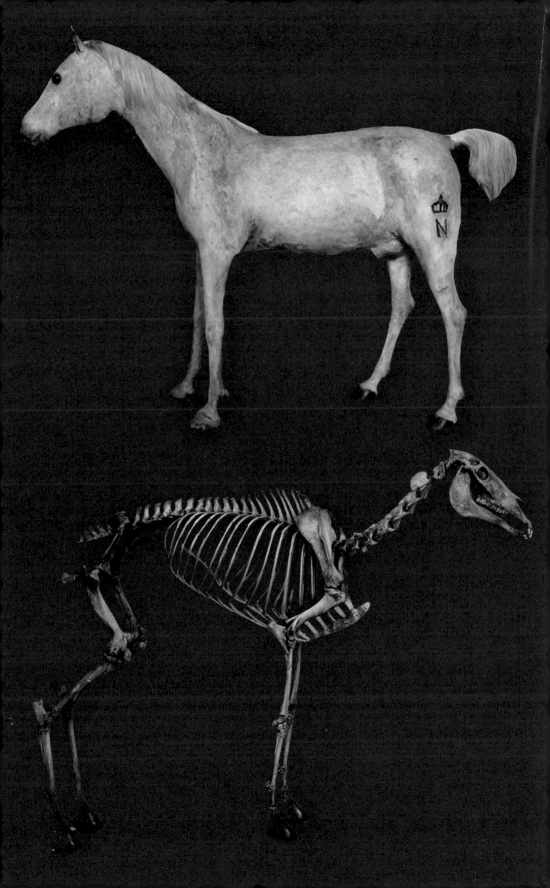

46

Le Vizir

NAPOLEON WAS APPARENTLY not a natural horse-man and his style of riding was far from classical, having learned to ride in Corsica, where bridles were usually bitless. In fact, Ernst Odeleben in 1813 described Napoleon's style of riding as

> like a butcher. He held the bridle in his right hand, with the left pendent. He looked as though he were suspended on his saddle. Whilst galloping, his body rolled backwards and forwards and sideways, according to the speed of his horse. As soon as the animal stepped aside, its rider lost his seat, and as we know Napoleon more than once was thrown.

However, given Napoleon's active lifestyle, his need for a large stable of horses was paramount. Napoleon did not like large horses and preferred small Arab horses, which were gentle natured, sturdy and responsive to commands.

Date of construction:
1829

Location:
Musée de l'Armée, Paris, France

At Waterloo Napoleon rode a grey Arab mare named Desiree, but two other of his horses remain to us today: Le Vizir (pictured top, left), which was stuffed and mounted and now resides at the Musée de l'Armée in Paris, and Marengo, the skeleton of which (pictured bottom, left) is now exhibited at the National Army Museum at Chelsea.

However, these may not be what they claim. Despite the fact that Napoleon had been Britain's most inveterate enemy, with his capture the British public seems to have fallen in love with him, despite referring to him as the 'Tyrant' and the 'Monster' only a few months before. Soon everyone wanted to read about nothing else, and the opportunity to see something associated with him was a thing not to miss. With the rise of Napoleomania, as it became known, there was clearly a great deal of money to be made.

There was certainly a horse in the imperial stable named Vizir and it seems likely, although it cannot be proven beyond doubt, that it was Napoleon's horse. It is claimed that Le Vizir was presented to Napoleon by the Sultan of the Ottoman Empire in 1808 and that it had died in 1829.

Le Vizir or Vizier only became known to the French people when the stuffed animal was exhibited to the Parisian public on 29 June 1868. It seems that the Natural History Society of Manchester had presented it to Napoleon's nephew, Napoleon III, who placed it in storage in the Louvre. How or when the Natural History Society had acquired it is a mystery, nor why they presented it to Napoleon III. There is, though, a record of the minutes of the society dated 25 January 1843 which records that 'the celebrated Arabian charger Vizier formerly property of Napoleon Buonaparte, presented by John Greaves, esq. Of Staffordshire, is an interesting relic of that extraordinary man, and has attracted the attention of many visitors.' How Mr Greaves had obtained the stuffed horse has never been established, nor the provenance of the horse confirmed.

But what of Marengo? A live white Arab charger was first exhibited at the Waterloo Rooms in London in 1823 as the star attraction. It was claimed that Marengo was named after the Battle of Marengo, through which he carried Napoleon. Marengo had apparently been imported to France from Egypt in 1799 as a 6-year-old. He was wounded eight times and reputedly carried the emperor in the battles of Austerlitz, Jena-Auerstedt, Wagram and Waterloo. As one of fifty-two horses in

BONAPARTE'S
White Barb CHARGER,
MARENGO,
Has been inspected by many of the Nobility and Gentry,
And is NOW EXHIBITING at the WATERLOO ROOMS,
No. 94, PALL MALL.

This beautiful white Barb Charger was the favourite Horse of the late Emperor, and accompanied him through most of his Battles. He has five Wounds which are visible; and a Bullet still remains in his Tail. The Imperial Crown and the Letter N are branded on his hind Quarters. He is so gentle, that the most timid Lady may approach him without fear.
The superb Saddle and Bridle and the Boots that Napoleon wore at Moscow, are likewise shown.
The Person who exhibits the Horse, is well acquainted with the Movements of the late Emperor, and speaks six different Languages.
Admittance, Ladies and Gentlemen, 1s. Children and Servants, 6d.

Napoleon's personal stud, Marengo apparently fled with the other horses when the stables were raided by Russians in 1812, and he survived the retreat from Moscow.

The stallion was reputedly captured in 1815 at the Battle of Waterloo and ownership soon transferred to a John Angerstein, the son of a City financier, whose superb art collection became the nucleus of the newly built National Gallery's collection. The horse saw out his life at the Angerstein stables and he died in 1832. The body of Marengo was sent to London Hospital to be articulated so that it could be put on public show. This was the same year that the body of the philospher Jeremy Bentham was articulated and put on display at University College London.

With the resurgence in interest in Napoleon when his body was returned to France from St Helena in 1840, great interest was suddenly shown in the remains of 'Marengo' as well. But many of the claims made regarding Marengo are hard to reconcile with the known facts. The imperial stable books list no horse named Marengo. It is very unlikely that a horse born in 1792/3, as claimed, could have survived until 1832. In fact, checking the skeleton's measurements against the imperial stables records reveals only one similarly sized horse – Ali, but he was recorded as being seven years younger. All in all it would seem that Marengo is probably a fake, with a manufactured name and history.

Another of Napoleon's horses, Jaffa, is known to have been brought back to Britain, by a Mr Green who purchased it at a Belgian auction after Waterloo, but this horse lived in relative obscurity at his owner's mansion in Kent. Jaffa had to be put down in 1829 and was buried at the estate with a memorial column erected over his grave stating, 'Under this stone lies Jaffa the charger of Napoleon aged 37 years'. The provenance of this claim is also impossible to establish.

47 Prussian Landwehr cap or *schirmutze*

OF THE PRUSSIAN troops engaged at Waterloo, fully half of the infantry and one-third of the cavalry engaged were not actually line troops, but designated 'Landwehr'. The German terms translates as 'defence of the country'.

The Prussian Landwehr, which saw extensive service from 1813–15, was first established in East Prussia, which was occupied by General Yorck's former Prussian Auxiliary Corps and declared to be at war with France on 7 February 1813. King Frederick Wilhelm II decreed the establishment of a militia or Landwehr throughout Prussia barely a month later, on 17 March 1813. This called up all men capable of bearing arms between the ages of 18 and 45, who were not already serving in the regular army, for the defence of the country.

Theoretically, the Landwehr were organised into brigades (regiments) of four battalions, of four companies of up to 200 men each. Few units achieved anywhere near this size, as there was a severe wastage of men from disease, straggling and enemy action over the course of the long campaign of 1813–14. By the end of the campaign, though, the Landwehr that remained were considered virtually equal to the line troops.

The Landwehr was allowed to return home at the end of the war in 1814 and disbanded. The new Landwehr formed hurriedly early in 1815 lacked their predecessors' experience and training. However, the force fought bravely in the battles of Ligny and Waterloo, their strengths being utilised in the ferocious and brutal close combat of Ligny and Plancenoit. Often in 1815 these troops carried British-supplied 'Brown Bess' muskets.

The Landwehr uniform consisted of a long, dark blue or black Litewka coat, with collar and cuffs in the colour of the provinces of West Prussia, Pomerania, Silesia, Neumark or Kurmark. A dark blue or black *schirmutze* cap was worn, again with a band of the provincial colour. The front of the cap was decorated with a white Landwehr cross, bearing the inscription *mit Gott für König und Vaterland 1813* ('For God, for King and the Fatherland 1813').

Much of the equipment supplied to the Landwehr was of poor quality and deteriorated rapidly on campaign, but the leather and brass version of the cap illustrated is of an unusually high quality.

Date of manufacture:
1813–15

Location:
Private collection

48 Drum of the 42nd Foot

COMMUNICATION OF ORDERS to the troops was paramount in Napoleonic battles such as Waterloo. The troops were required to manoeuvre in tightly packed formation in perfect time, and the exigencies of combat required this to be achieved accurately and quickly.

The immediate method of communicating orders was by word of mouth. The senior officer, established behind the centre of the battalion, bellowed out the order and this was repeated along the line by the officers of each company. However, this took time, could easily be disrupted by enemy fire and might be difficult to hear or understand clearly during the confusion and

Date of construction:
c. 1815

Location:
National Army Museum, London, UK

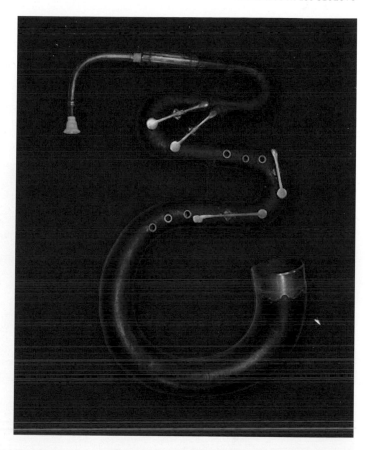

Serpent owned by drummer Richard Bentinck, 23rd Foot, inscribed for his services at Waterloo

din of battle. To counteract this, musical instruments were used to pass orders quickly and clearly, particularly drums for infantry units and bugles in light infantry and cavalry units, with each specific drum roll or bugle call denoting a specific command.

Such humble beginnings led to some colonels of regiments setting up complete bands, to encourage the men and to help maintain the pace when marching long distances. French regiments even occasionally had poles with bells attached, which the British named 'Jingling Johnnies'.

Such additional musicians, as today, became less essential in the heat of battle and reverted to a more vital role of helping wounded comrades to the surgical posts just behind the front lines, where they could be initially accessed and possibly treated. They were not trained to any medical standard, but acted as bearers.

49 French dragoon helmet

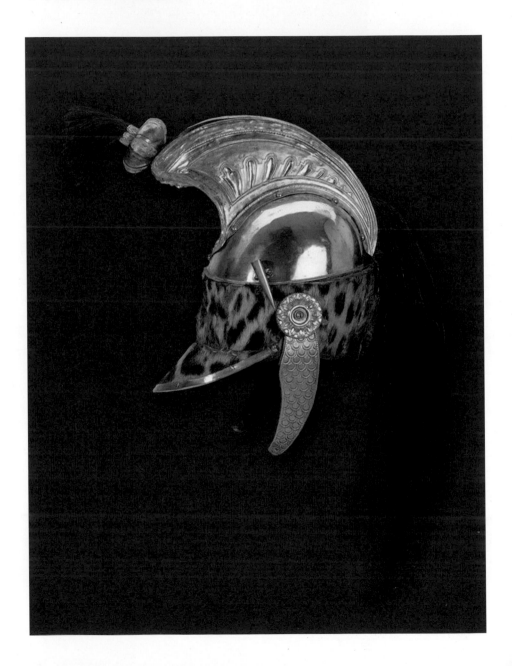

THIS DRAGOON HELMET is made entirely of brass, giving a great deal less protection than the iron skull cap of the cuirassiers. The heavy cavalry were the key strike force of any army, used as the main shock force to smash through the enemy lines. These cavalry were known under numerous titles: guard cavalry, cuirassiers, carabiniers and dragoons, but were generally dressed and armed similarly except for the cuirassiers and carabiniers, who wore body armour (see item 10).

These cavalrymen universally carried heavy swords which were straight bladed as shown, not curved slashing swords like the light cavalry. These weapons could be used to slash at an enemy, but were generally designed to be used to thrust, with the sword point stabbing the enemy.

Most heavy cavalry were also equipped with muskets; it is recorded that French dragoons would sometimes dismount and act as infantry, using their dragoon muskets.

The British heavy cavalry was largely a spent force after its use in the defeat of d'Erlon's corps and subsequent mauling by the French lancers. This gave Napoleon a great advantage, with his heavy cavalry still in perfect order in reserve. However, these heavy cavalry regiments were swallowed up in the mass French cavalry attacks against the allied infantry squares. In the end the light cavalry decided the battle: the French collapse released the British light cavalry to destroy any last semblances of resistance and the Prussian light cavalry to decimate the routing French during the night that followed.

Date of manufacture:
c. 1815

Location:
National Army Museum, London, UK

French cuirassier sword.

50 Livret

Date of production: 1814

Location: National Library of Scotland, Edinburgh, Scotland

TO MAINTAIN HIS armies, Napoleon introduced conscription by lot on 28 December 1803, and each year names were selected at a lottery of all eligible men in each town and city to meet the number of army conscripts required under the Act. This system was deemed

Rare depiction of the dead on the Waterloo battlefield

more democratic as all classes of society could be drawn, although there were many exemptions and ways of personally avoiding service by supplying a substitute.

Every soldier in the French army was issued with his *livret* or pocket book, which contained details of his service and equipment issues. The particular booklet pictured was collected from the battlefield and had been issued to Louis Monsigny, a farmer from Boulogne who joined the 43ème Régiment de Ligne in 1814, which was not actually at Waterloo.

Further information contained in the livret was:

Name of mother and father
Date of any marriage
Size, including back length, length of the arms,
    crotch length, belt size, head size, leg length
Equipment provided: greatcoat, trousers, cap,
    shako or helmet, boots, shoes or leggings
Dates of vaccinations against smallpox
Level of education and qualifications if appropriate
    (e.g. swimmer)
Statements of military training
Campaigns served in
Dates of service
Injuries and oustanding actions, citations and
    decorations
Promotions
Permissions (e.g. to get married)

The battlefield after Waterloo is almost always described by eyewitnesses as being littered with papers; these were invariably the soldiers' livrets, which were often disturbed by pillagers searching the pockets of the dead and wounded during the dreadful night after the fighting was over.

51 French caisson

THE RESUPPLY OF ammunition was as vitally important to the armies at Waterloo as it is to any army in
combat operations today. It was the role of the commis-
sary to transport ammunition to supply depots but the
responsibility of the artillery to carry spare ammunition
on the battlefield for both the artillery and the infantry. A typical caisson for a 12-pounder would carry 48
rounds of ball, whereas a 6-pounder carried around
140 rounds.

Each army had its own versions of ammunition
carts, or caissons, but all were sturdy covered wagons
with additional features incorporated to try to avoid fire
reaching the gunpowder charges. Although the round
shot and the musket balls themselves were inert, they
were pre-manufactured in packages which included the
gunpowder required for ease of firing. These were lined
up in a pre-made sectional system within the cart.

**Date of
construction:**
c. 1815

Location:
Les Invalides,
Paris, France

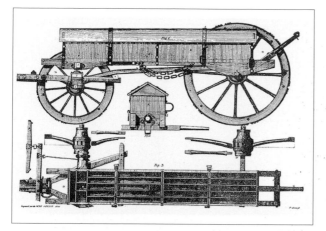

Drawing of a caisson.

This made the carts extremely dangerous and for this reason, the caissons assigned to batteries were, as far as possible, parked in a dip of the ground some way in the rear of the battery they served, sheltered from much of the enemy fire. Infantry units would keep a wide berth as well – the threat of a large explosion was deemed too great.

Resupplying the armies at Waterloo with reserve ammunition during the battle was difficult, stressful and hazardous, but not impossible. Claims that the Brussels road was completely blocked are exaggerated, and many eyewitnesses confirm that ammunition wagons were seen moving up to the army along this road throughout the day and subsequent night to resupply the army before it marched into France.

Many of the personnel of the reserve artillery units, which were not able to be fully formed before the campaign began, were utilised to provide additional staff for the ammunition resupply and many, although not all, received a Waterloo medal in recognition of their work.

A number of caissons received direct hits during the battle and several exploded, causing many casualties to neighbouring units. However, the most tragic deaths occurred when careless marauders attempted to break into caissons after the battle, hoping to discover valuables. One such pair of British infantrymen caused a spark as they broke the lock off an abandoned caisson and a huge explosion ensued. Both were thrown high into the air and fell to earth barely alive; every stitch of their clothing had been blasted away and their skin was horribly scorched. Their last few hours were undoubtedly ones of great agony, at a time when morphine did not exist.

52

Hotel
d'Hane-Steenhuyse

IN 1815, THE French king, Louis XVIII, having been forced to flee Paris as Napoleon approached, made his way towards Lille and then crossed the Belgian border. He went to Ghent, possibly remembering that the aristocrat Comte Emmanuel Ignace d'Hane had received him very graciously when he had been the mere Comte de Provence.

The comte received the king with great cordiality and he allowed Louis to use his ground-floor apartments as his court in exile, whilst the d'Hane family continued to live on the first floor. The original medieval buildings had been destroyed and a Baroque-style frontage was added in 1767, with an elegant neo-classic garden front in 1773. The ballroom is small but beautifully decorated and reaches the whole height of the building. Here Louis regularly held balls and levees. Leading off the ballroom is a reception room, where he would receive the dignitaries of Europe and routinely met the officers of every British regiment as they marched through Ghent on their way from Ostend to join the army around Brussels. Another room off from the other side of the ballroom is the room that Louis used as both his study and bedroom.

The entire front of the house is taken up by the 'green room', named after the colour of the drapes and seat

Date of construction:
1698

Location:
Ghent, Belgium

cushions. This was Louis' dining room; it was normal for French sovereigns to dine in public and the great wooden shutters were opened for the world to watch from the street as the king and his entourage ate and drank in style. He was generally renowned for his corpulence, but showed a quick wit and intelligence.

Few histories of the campaign actually consider what occurred at Ghent when the alarming news of Napoleon's invasion was received and what happened to the fledgling French Royalist army that was being formed at Alost under the command of the Duc de Berri during the campaign.

At the beginning of June 1815, Ghent was teeming with troops, although a number were of doubtful ability. Major General Lambert's British Brigade was stationed there, as were a number of very newly raised Belgian militia battalions. On the morning of 16 June, the letter written the previous evening by the Duke of Wellington to the French minister for war, the Duc de Feltre, arrived in Ghent. A copy of this was immediately forwarded to the Duc de Berri at Alost.

Rumours of heavy defeats and of Wellington's army being routed continued to filter in throughout the ensuing day, further disturbing the populace. The order for Lambert's troops to march to join the army inflamed the tense situation. However, Louis XVIII appears to have remained firm within all of this chaos; as Comte Rouchechouart later recalled:

> The Duc de Feltre ... Took me to the king; we found him surrounded by people urging him to save himself. Louis XVIII, calm and resigned, replied 'Gentlemen, I have not received official news and if the reversal is as great as you say, I should have been informed. I will not leave here unless I am forced by circumstances; those who are afraid should leave.'

Many of the populace, including the entire Belgian militia were not so stoical; they fled en masse for Antwerp and beyond, abandoning their equipment along the roads.

The ballroom.

At Alost, the Duc de Berri, commanding the Royalist army, immediately ordered his forces to form up, but within minutes he had despatched a letter to his father, the Comte d'Artois, at Ghent, advising him to leave the city immediately. Clearly believing many of these rumours of defeat and disaster, de Berri had already decided to retire with his force to Termonde, behind the protection of the river Scheldt. Within a couple of hours the Royalist army had left Alost in great haste, leaving only a handful of cavalry to guard the place.

The only one to retain his dignity was Louis XVIII, who trusted Wellington and refused to flee without just cause. Wellington repaid this trust by inviting Louis to follow the armies into France and he was able to reclaim his throne without opposition – something the other allies were not enthusiastic about.

This little gem of an historic building hides in plain sight on one of the busiest streets in the city of Ghent. The archaic organisation required to arrange a visit to view its interiors may be the root cause of this obscurity, but it is well worth the effort.

53 French Louis d'or

THIS COIN, ALTHOUGH bearing the head of Louis XVIII, was actually minted in London in 1815. It is believed that the coins were minted with the consent of Louis, to pay the allied troops whilst on French soil. It is reputed that Nathan Rothschild suggested the measure as he found it impossible to supply the army with French coin to purchase goods when in France.

The Louis d'or was a 20-franc piece of 90 per cent gold. Around £1.5 million of gold and silver were allocated to the mint to produce these coins and Thomas Wyon, who also designed the Waterloo medal, produced dies with which to strike the coins, which looked exactly like the French versions and matched their fineness.

Some of these coins inevitably found their way into circulation in Paris, which caused great alarm to the authorities and occasioned an exchange of diplomatic letters with the French, who deemed them as counterfeit. The minting of the coins was stopped in November 1815, but by then over 871,000 of them had been issued to the army and had entered circulation.

As was standard practice in France, coins were minted at several locations, the location of the mint being shown on the reverse of the coin to the right of the date of issue. At the height of the French Empire there had been twenty mints, each with a specific identifying letter, from A for Paris, through II for La Rochelle to CL for Genoa; London had taken the letter R, as can be seen in the image, L having already been allocated to Bayonne.

The theory that these coins were produced to flood the France economy with counterfeit money to destroy its economy are wide of the mark, Louis would never have acceded to such a destructive policy.

Date of production:
1815

Location:
Private collection

54 British 5½-inch howitzer

EVERY BATTERY AT Waterloo had six or eight guns, at least one of which was a howitzer rather than a cannon. Uniquely one battery, Captain Bull's Horse Artillery Troop, was equipped solely with six howitzers.

Cannon had a long barrel and, although the barrel could be elevated a little above the horizontal to increase the range by a screw arrangement, their fire was still restricted to a horizontal trajectory. Their effective range was around 900 metres with solid ball, although they could ricochet much further on hard ground.

The howitzer, however, had a much shorter and chubbier barrel which could fire horizontally, but it was also

Date of manufacture:
1815

Location:
Firepower Museum, Woolwich, UK

possible to elevate the barrel to a much higher angle, nearer the vertical than horizontal. This allowed the howitzer to perform in ways conventional cannon could not – in particular it could fire over intervening obstacles to reach troops behind buildings, woods or hills. These shells could effectively be lobbed around 800 metres.

It did, however, require a great deal of experience to set the fuse perfectly, so that it did not burst too high to have the desired effect or burn too long that it either buried itself in the mud or had the fuse snuffed out by a very courageous recipient. Throughout the battle, there are mentions of shells falling to earth and burying themselves in the soft Belgian mud and then exploding harmlessly, splashing those around with the liquid mud.

Bull's troop played a significant role against the French troops attacking Hougoumont through the wood. Indeed, this troop has been credited with driving back a number of the French attacks by its concentrated fire of shrapnel shells, which tore through the French infantry.

French howitzers were also used against Hougoumont, using carcass, which was an iron ball filled with highly combustible material and these succeeded in setting fire to the château and the great barn.

55 Magnifying glass

owned by Lieutenant Colonel the Honourable Alexander Gordon, 3rd Foot Guards

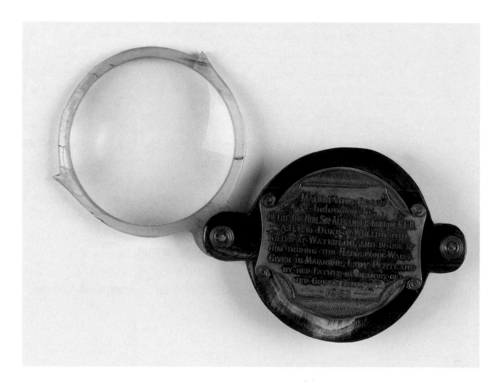

ALEXANDER GORDON WAS the third son of George Gordon, Lord Haddo. His brothers were prime minister George Hamilton-Gordon, the fourth Earl of Aberdeen, and Sir Robert Gordon, a diplomat.

Alexander had joined the army in Spain during the Battle of Corunna in 1808 as aide-de-camp to his uncle, General Sir David Baird. He then became aide-de-camp to the Duke of Wellington for the next six years.

Gordon received brevet (acting rank) promotions to major and lieutenant colonel as rewards for carrying home the despatches announcing the victories of the

Date of manufacture: c. 1815

Location: National Army Museum, London, UK

The bed in which
Gordon died.

Battle of Corunna and the siege of Ciudad Rodrigo.

He was wounded at the Battle of Waterloo at about 7 p.m. while rallying some Brunswickers and was carried from the field on a door by a group of soldiers. Surgeon John Hume encountered this group as they left the field and he immediately inspected the wound. A musket ball had entered Gordon's left thigh and damaged the artery and shattered his femur. He was losing a great deal of blood and Hume, assisted by Dr Matthias Kenny of the artillery, amputated the leg in the field.

After the operation, Gordon was carried back to Wellington's headquarters at Waterloo (see item 20). He complained continually of the wound, and the stump was at one point reopened to remove a quantity of congealed blood. He died in Hume's arms at about 3 a.m. on 19 June.

Hume describes how he went upstairs and tapped on the duke's door. The duke had undressed but had not washed himself; as Hume entered, he sat up and held Hume's hand as Hume recounted the death of poor Gordon and the names of other senior officers who were dead or severely wounded. The duke was apparently much affected and Hume felt tears dropping onto his hand. Wellington suddenly brushed the tears away and said with a great deal of emotion, ' Well, thank God, I don't know what it is to lose a battle; but certainly nothing can be more painful than to gain one with the loss of so many of one's friends.'

There is a monument to Gordon on the field close to La Haye Sainte, on what now appears to be a small knoll. In fact this knoll is the last vestige of the true height of the allied ridge at this point, before huge amounts of earth were removed after the battle to form the Lion Mound (see item 95).

56 Czapka of the Red Lancers

THIS TRADITIONAL POLISH helmet, or czapka, with its square top is actually from 2ème Régiment de Chevau-légers Lanciers de la Garde Impériale, more often known as the 'Red Lancers', which was formed in 1810 from the Royal Dutch Guard light cavalry, when the Kingdom of Holland was annexed by France. When the regiment was formed it was given a new scarlet uniform which replicated the traditional Polish lancer's uni-

form. The regiment was commanded by Colonel Baron Pierre de Colbert-Chabanais, under whom it gained a fearsome reputation.

The front rank only carried the lance, which in dexterous hands was very effective, as it outreached the length of a musket with bayonet attached. The rear rank carried a sword, which was more easy to wield in close combat and avoided injuries to the man in front. Although seen as a deadly weapon, especially to unformed troops, there are numerous accounts of infantrymen sus-

Lance head.

taining as many as twenty-three lance wounds and surviving. However, all of the French lancers gained a fearsome reputation for showing no mercy at all, rarely, if ever, taking prisoners, and they are often cited as guilty of finishing off wounded men lying on the battlefield as they passed.

The regiment went to Russia in 1812 and was decimated during the terrible retreat, leaving very few surviving members of the original Dutch corps that had formed it. The numbers were replenished with Frenchmen and when Napoleon returned from Elba, the regiment marched with the Imperial Guard into Belgium with an additional squadron of Polish lancers – the last vestiges of the 1st Regiment of Lancers of the Guards known as the 'Sacred Squadron' who had gone to Elba with Napoleon under Chef d'Escadron Jerzmanowski. This squadron was attached, but was given seniority over the Red Lancers.

On 15 June the regiment advanced with Ney's left wing of the army, skirmishing with Dutch troops at Frasnes, whilst the Polish squadron rode round the town and apparently got very close to the crossroads of Quatre Bras. The role of the Red Lancers at the Battle of Quatre Bras is unclear, although many British eyewitnesses claim that the infantry square of the 42nd was attacked by them.

Date of manufacture:
c. 1812 15

Location:
Musée de l'Armée, Paris, France

At Waterloo, the regiment appears to have remained in reserve until the mass cavalry attacks against the allied squares. However, many witnesses from the Scots Greys claim to have been attacked by the Red Lancers during their charge, losing heavily to their lances. The regiment spent its force in the failed attacks against the squares, but did support the Imperial Guard in its final attack, before joining the rout.

57 Case containing musket ball
that killed George Holmes, and one of his vertebrae

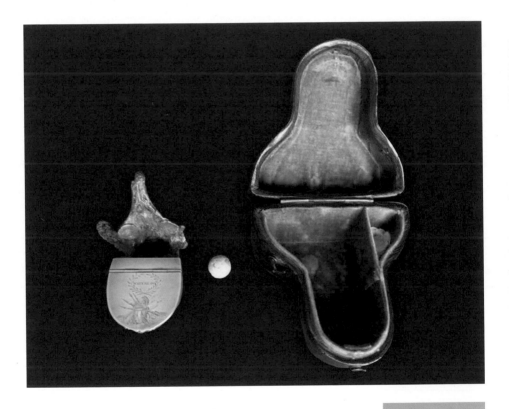

THE 27TH FOOT (Inniskillings) stood in reserve throughout most of the battle, but after the fall of La Haye Sainte they were forced to stand in square in the front line because of the threat from French cavalry, while being decimated by cannon fire and close-range musket fire. The battalion numbered 750 men before the battle but had 105 men killed and 373 men wounded – a total of 478 casualties in only a few hours. The square

Date of production:
1815

Location:
Private collection

of corpses was apparently very distinct on the battlefield the next day.

Captain George Holmes of the 27th Foot was killed by a ball during the battle, and legend has it that he may have been killed by one of his own company, presumably by accident. However, it is clear that the ball is too small to be a musket ball and is more likely to be a pistol ball or from case shot. Holmes must have died of his wounds and his body operated upon post mortem for the ball and the vertebra to have been extracted for his widow as macabre keepsakes. It is odd that there is no record of his burial – his body may well have simply been added to a mass grave.

One eyewitness claims to have seen the corpse of a grey-haired officer of the Inniskillings lying face down on the battlefield with much of his face and skull missing, torn away by a cannon shot. It has been assumed by many that he describes Holmes but it is more likely to be the corpse of Ensign Samuel Ireland, who had previously been a sergeant major in the regiment.

On 1 November 1815 a court martial was held on Captain John Tucker of the Inniskillings, who had been severely wounded in the abdomen and recuperated in Brussels. Amongst a number of charges, he was accused of having broken open the portmanteau, trunk and canteen of George Holmes and disposing of his clothes, money and effects. He was further charged with burning or destroying the letters and papers of Captain Holmes, including the private and regimental accounts at his Brussels property. Tucker was eventually found not guilty of these charges but found guilty of others and dismissed the service. He was, however, allowed to transfer to the 8th Foot, but quit the service in 1816.

58

Coatee of Surgeon Samuel Good

EACH BATTALION OF infantry was usually supplied with two surgeons to tend to the wounded of the battalion who wore a red jacket as depicted, making him somewhat difficult to differentiate from a combatant. These surgeons would set up a hasty field dressing station in a more protected spot just to the rear, where they and their charges would be out of danger from musket or cannonballs. Here they would provide emergency surgery and then arrange to have the wounded transported to a hospital.

The sheer numbers of wounded at Waterloo overwhelmed the battalion surgeons and the walking wounded often made their way to Mont St Jean or even Waterloo village in search of a surgeon.

In addition to the regimental surgeons, a number of senior surgeons were appointed to the Staff; these provided a further tranche of surgeons who were available to staff Mont St Jean as a field hospital for all-comers. Although Samuel Good was the senior surgeon attached to the 2nd Battalion 3rd Guards which fought in Hougoumont orchard for most of the day, the battalion unusually had two assistant surgeons as well. Probably because of this, Samuel Good was seconded to Mont St Jean Farm, where he performed surgery all day and late into the night.

Date of manufacture:
c. 1815

Location:
Edinburgh Surgeons' Hall, Edinburgh, Scotland

Surgery was still relatively rudimentary in modern terms, for without the ability to administer anaesthetics, sedation, blood transfusions, sterile dressings or antiseptics, the surgeons were very limited in what they could achieve. Wounds to the torso, where organs were damaged, could rarely be operated on and the patient had to be left to recover slowly or die a slow agonising death. With wounds to the head, trepanning had been perfected as an operation to relieve pressure on the brain, but beyond that it was largely up to the patient again to recover or, more likely, succumb. Surgery was possible for wounds to any of the limbs and generally offered a reasonably high success rate if performed soon after the injury. Flesh wounds could be simply sewn up and musket balls embedded in muscle extracted with a probe – an uncomfortable operation without painkillers. Breaks in the bones of the leg or arm, if simple, could be set and allowed to heal naturally. However, often the musket or cannonball shattered and splintered the bone and a repair was impossible. The surgeon's only answer to this was amputation.

Techniques for amputations had improved dramatically during the Napoleonic wars and most would be expected to survive such an operation. It had been found that the body's nervous system essentially shut down for up to twelve hours after such a traumatic injury and it was therefore a priority to carry out the operation as soon as possible; with luck this also reduced the threat of gangrene.

Historically amputations had been a simple straight cut through the muscle and bone, but this left the bone hard up against the stump and made wearing a prosthetic leg uncomfortable. Therefore, the operation usually entailed three cuts: the first severed all of the nerve endings of the skin, then the muscle was cut away to the bone at an angle to create an inverted cone; finally the muscle was drawn back with the aid of bandages and the bone cut through as high up as could be reached. Once released, this allowed the arteries to be tied off and the muscle flaps to be sewn together to form a soft pad, ideal for fitting prosthetics.

Plate showing the two methods of amputating a limb.

It is estimated that 9 per cent of Waterloo campaign patients who reached a hospital later succumbed to their wounds, with around 80 per cent eventually returning to their units or veteran battalions. This loss rate is actually higher than that achieved during the later battles of the Peninsular War, where death rates were as low as 5 per cent, but this was almost certainly partly to do with the lack of experienced surgeons – many Peninsular surgeons being in Canada – and the inordinate time it took some of the injured to be collected from the battlefield.

59 The Battle of Waterloo by a Near Observer

WITHIN MONTHS OF the Battle of Waterloo, publishing history was made by a book which sought to supply the public with details of the battle in a way never seen before. It was published anonymously by a 'Near Observer' by the publisher John Booth of London and is often therefore referred to as Booth's history of the battle. It was an overnight success, having ten editions published within the first three years and it continued to be reprinted in various guises well into the 1840s.

The book consists of a narrative of the campaign, the official accounts from all countries involved, letters from eyewitnesses, biographical sketches of the fallen and details of honours conferred on individuals. It was also superbly illustrated with images of battle scenes by George Jones,

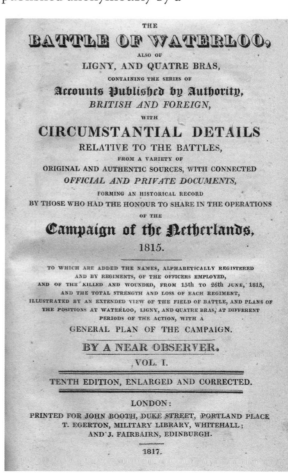

THE

BATTLE OF WATERLOO,

ALSO OF

LIGNY, AND QUATRE BRAS,

CONTAINING THE SERIES OF

Accounts Published by Authority,

BRITISH AND FOREIGN,

WITH

CIRCUMSTANTIAL DETAILS

RELATIVE TO THE BATTLES,

FROM A VARIETY OF

ORIGINAL AND AUTHENTIC SOURCES, WITH CONNECTED

OFFICIAL AND PRIVATE DOCUMENTS,

FORMING AN HISTORICAL RECORD

BY THOSE WHO HAD THE HONOUR TO SHARE IN THE OPERATIONS

OF THE

Campaign of the Netherlands,

1815.

TO WHICH ARE ADDED THE NAMES, ALPHABETICALLY REGISTERED
AND BY REGIMENTS, OF THE OFFICERS EMPLOYED,
AND OF THE KILLED AND WOUNDED, FROM 15th TO 26th JUNE, 1815,
AND THE TOTAL STRENGTH AND LOSS OF EACH REGIMENT,
ILLUSTRATED BY AN EXTENDED VIEW OF THE FIELD OF BATTLE, AND PLANS OF
THE POSITIONS AT WATERLOO, LIGNY, AND QUATRE BRAS, AT DIFFERENT
PERIODS OF THE ACTION, WITH A

GENERAL PLAN OF THE CAMPAIGN.

BY A NEAR OBSERVER.

VOL. I.

TENTH EDITION, ENLARGED AND CORRECTED.

LONDON:

PRINTED FOR JOHN BOOTH, DUKE STREET, PORTLAND PLACE
T. EGERTON, MILITARY LIBRARY, WHITEHALL;
AND J. FAIRBAIRN, EDINBURGH.

1817.

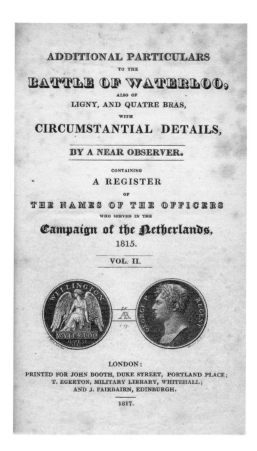

ADDITIONAL PARTICULARS
TO THE
BATTLE OF WATERLOO,
ALSO OF
LIGNY, AND QUATRE BRAS,
WITH
CIRCUMSTANTIAL DETAILS,
BY A NEAR OBSERVER.
CONTAINING
A REGISTER
OF
THE NAMES OF THE OFFICERS
WHO SERVED IN THE
Campaign of the Netherlands,
1815.

VOL. II.

LONDON:
PRINTED FOR JOHN BOOTH, DUKE STREET, PORTLAND PLACE;
T. EGERTON, MILITARY LIBRARY, WHITEHALL;
AND J. FAIRBAIRN, EDINBURGH.

1817.

The rarer Volume II.

Date of printing:
1815

Location:
Private collection

excellent maps and a marvellous 360-degree view of the battlefield from a spot just north of La Haye Sainte.

The much rarer second volume contained additional eyewitness accounts and maps and rounded off with returns of the killed and wounded and lists of all British officers present.

The whole project was an original concept and wonderfully executed – by a woman. The 'Near Observer' has been proven to be one Charlotte Waldie, who later wrote an account of her own circumstances and the events she witnessed whilst living in Brussels during the Waterloo campaign entitled *Narrative of a Residence in Belgium, during the Campaign of 1815, and of a Visit to the Field of Waterloo by an Englishwoman*, which was published in 1817 and itself has seen a number of reprints under various titles.

Charlotte was the daughter of a regional banker and a budding writer of travel books. She happened to be in Brussels with her brother John and sister Jane when the campaign began, but she saw immediately the potential of such a significant victory and within days she was interviewing the wounded and collecting material for the book.

Her sister Jane was an accomplished artist and it was she who produced the wonderful view of the battlefield shortly after the battle, before it was marred by the numerous memorials and altered markedly by the construction of the Lion Mound. Sadly, Jane died young in 1826.

Charlotte married a banker named Stephen Eaton in 1822 and continued publishing works under her married name and died aged 70 in 1859.

60

Brick from Hougoumont garden wall

Date of manufacture:
Seventeenth century

Location:
Private collection

AS THE FRENCH troops marched through the wood at Hougoumont, their view was so obstructed by the foliage that the château was probably unknown to them.

Much has been made of the defence of this farmstead, but because of the high buildings with blind walls that formed most of the outer walls of this ad hoc fortress, there were few places from which the occupying troops could actually engage the French attacks unless they broke in (see item 22). The troops could fire in limited numbers from the windows of the gardener's house which stood across the southern gateway, although two of the window spaces directly above the gate, as at present, were bricked up well before the fighting and could not be used. Troops could also fire over the gardener's house from the top room of the château, but at long and therefore very inaccurate range.

However, on the southern and eastern side, a formal Belgian garden was enclosed by a 7ft high red brick wall. With the use of quickly constructed wooden or earthen firing steps, the defenders could look over the wall to fire and then quickly drop back down into cover to reload whilst another took his turn to fire. This was also supplemented by knocking small holes through the bricks to form loopholes to fire through.

The garden walls were lined variously by men of the Coldstream and 3rd Guards and also by Nassau troops, according to their commander Busgen, particularly after their troops were relieved in their previous defence of the gardener's house. The wood ended some 30 yards from the southern wall, forming a corridor of open land without cover which the French troops had to cross to get to the wall. This strip of land, some 200 yards long, became a veritable killing ground as the defenders could fire at any attack along the entire length of this wall.

Many French troops avoided crossing this void, lining the edge of the wood, which accorded some cover, from where they attempted to pick off the defenders as they briefly bobbed into view to take aim and fire. There is a good deal of evidence that some French marksmen actually climbed into the trees on the edge of the wood in an attempt to fire over the wall. The gate between the southern courtyard and the garden was deemed a fatal spot by the defenders, which confirms this theory, as the French could only have been seen this place if they were at a significant elevation above ground level.

The eastern wall overlooked an adjoining orchard which was fought over intensely throughout the battle. French troops advancing through this orchard were under heavy fire from their front, with the defenders lining a 'sunken way' which bordered the northern edge of the orchard. The defenders along the eastern wall therefore provided a heavy flanking fire which seriously disrupted French attempts to capture it.

It was vital that the orchard was not lost, because the northern boundary of the formal garden was not walled, but lined by a thick hedge. It would undoubtedly have not been beyond the capabilities of the French to break into the formal garden from here and although this would not have guaranteed the conquest of the farmstead, it certainly would have severely limited its defensive capabilities.

The formal garden is long gone – it is now merely a meadow – as has the large wood and orchard which surrounded it. However, the wall, which was recently decaying badly, is being repaired as part of the works for the 200th anniversary of the battle in 2015. The loopholes still exist; the white stones inserted as lintels were put in as part of the repairs after the battle, but help to delineate the loopholes for visitors.

61

Tarleton helmet

THE TARLETON HELMET, consisting of a leather skullcap with a large fur crest, was named after Sir Banastre Tarleton who had led a British cavalry force known as Tarleton's Legion in the American War of Independence. It became popular with all light infantry, but had fallen out of favour with all but the Royal Horse Artillery way before Waterloo.

Second Captain Alexander Cavalié Mercer, who reputedly wore this very helmet at Waterloo, wrote a journal of the Waterloo campaign, probably the greatest journal of a military campaign ever written. Although Mercer was second-in-command, he commanded G Troop Royal Horse Artillery at the battle because its actual commander, Lieutenant Colonel Alexander Dickson, was seconded to command the Battering Train.

The horse artillery differed from foot artillery in that every gunner was mounted, allowing the entire battery of guns to be manoeuvred into position with great speed, whereas the gunners in foot artillery units walked and thus moved much more slowly.

Mercer's troop did not arrive in time to take part in the action at Quatre Bras and he is honest in admitting the numerous mistakes he made in this sudden and unexpected march. The troop was fully involved with the cavalry in covering the retreat of Wellington's

Date of manufacture:
c. 1815

Location:
Private collection

191

army to the position of Waterloo, at one time firing upon Napoleon and his entourage and almost being captured at Genappe.

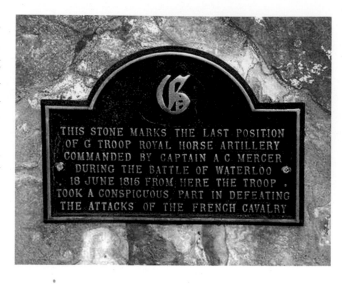

G Troop was held in reserve initially on 18 June and then deployed on the extreme right wing when it was feared that Napoleon's cavalry might try to pass around that flank. Finally, at around 4 p.m., the troop was rushed into the maelstrom of the battle, being placed on the ridge line in front of some Brunswick troops. Mercer had been sent forward to bolster the line of cannon against the French cavalry attacks, with orders for the men to abandon the guns and to seek shelter in the adjacent squares when the French pushed home their charges.

Plaque commemorating the site of Mercer's battery on the ridge line at Waterloo.

Mercer claims that the Brunswick troops looked too uneasy to stand firm if they saw his men abandon the guns. He therefore chose to disobey orders and to continue to man his guns. Loading his cannon with canister rounds and firing at the waves of French cavalry at very close range, he delivered a devastating fire which carved swathes through the tightly packed formation, the balls tearing into both men and horses. The six guns, firing every thirty seconds, simply mowed the cavalrymen down and soon a wall of human and equine flesh formed a barrier to the easy advance of further waves.

Recent research has shown that, although in essence Mercer's description of the battle is correct, it has certainly been overstated. The specific deaths and injuries of the men that Mercer describes are verifiable, but his more general claims that two-thirds of his men and 140 horses were *hors de combat* by the end of the battle do not tally with his own official returns. These show that

A rather fanciful depiction of Mercer's troop in action at Waterloo.

five men were killed and twenty men wounded; and that sixty-nine horses were killed or wounded. Clearly a number of unwounded would be temporarily missing, escorting wounded colleagues to the rear or simply making themselves scarce, but even these would not add up to the numbers Mercer claims were missing. It is also strange that no other eyewitness to the battle – either French or allied – remarked on the wall of flesh in the aftermath of the battle.

Further claims that he was under a devastating flank fire from a Prussian battery and was only saved by the supporting fire of a Netherlands battery, whose men he claims were all drunk, have been proven to be wrong. The battery enfilading his has been shown to be one of the French Imperial Guard which accompanied the final attack of the Guards, and the slur on Krahmer's battery would appear to be unfounded and vindictive.

Mercer's later correspondence, recently published, shows a man who remained very bitter because he felt that he was never accorded the recognition he deserved in the form of awards or promotion for the actions of his troop at Waterloo. His journal should be read and enjoyed with this proviso in mind.

62 18-pounder iron cannonball

THIS CAST-IRON cannonball was discovered in the ground near Waterloo village. Its sheer size is impressive. It weighs 18lb (12kg), three times the size of a 6-pounder ball, which is itself about the size of a shot putt. Because of its size and the kinetic energy imparted to it, it travelled much further and contained a much greater destructive power than the smaller ball.

The 18-pounder cannon was also much heavier, with a huge and unwieldy carriage that required a much

Date of manufacture:
c. 1815

Location:
Author's collection

larger horse team to manoeuvre it. For all these reasons cannon of this size were used almost exclusively for siege warfare, where they were sited in prepared positions to batter the walls down. As such these guns followed the army and were denoted as belonging to the Battering Train.

In 1815 Lieutenant Colonel Alexander Dickson, who had commanded the artillery in the Peninsular War, was in command of the Battering Train. Very unusually, three British 18-pounder batteries were in preparation to join the army when Napoleon invaded; these cannon were not attached to the Battering Train but were attached to the army reserve and so it would seem that Wellington had the idea of using them in pre-prepared defensive positions in the allied line. Such heavy cannon would have significantly increased the weight of firepower of the allied line and would have had a profound effect on the French forces as they advanced against Wellington's line.

The batteries were not ready to be used as they were lacking any drivers for the horse teams and were therefore re-embarked on barges to remove them from danger. This cannonball would appear to have been left behind by one of these batteries.

Many of these personnel were reassigned to the duties of aiding the resupply of artillery ammunition to the front line at the Battle of Waterloo. This has highlighted an anomaly in the distribution of the Waterloo Medal, as some of these men appear to have received the medal whilst others did not.

63

Church of St Catherine

ARRIVING NEAR THE battlefield, Blücher became aware that Wellington's army was under intense pressure and he became concerned that they were close to being beaten. Blücher therefore decided not to wait for additional forces to arrive, but to launch an immediate attack with his IV Corps under von Bülow upon the village of Plancenoit, which stood in Napoleon's right rear. The village, which in 1815 numbered about 500 inhabitants, was in the low ground of the Lasne stream and straggled up the slowly rising slope towards La Belle Alliance, some 1,400 yards (1,300m) away. The capture of the village would threaten Napoleon's right and give Prussian cannon command over the main road to Genappe, making it possible for them to fire at the French reserve formations. The Prussians captured most of the village, which was not initially garrisoned in force by the French, at around 4.30 p.m.

Date of construction:
The original thirteenth-century church was rebuilt in 1857

Location:
Plancenoit, Belgium

Lieutenant General Lobau's French VI Army Corps counter-attacked at Plancenoit in an effort to drive the Prussians back. Napoleon, learning that Plancenoit was in danger of being taken, sent his eight battalions of the Young Guard to reinforce Lobau.

Each was desperate to gain complete control of the village, and losses were high on both sides in the merciless hand-to-hand fighting which centred particularly around the walled churchyard of Plancenoit Church. No quarter was offered nor requested, and even the wounded were routinely slaughtered mercilessly by both sides. After extremely fierce fighting the Young Guard managed to recapture Plancenoit, only to be counter-attacked and slowly driven out again.

Napoleon then sent two battalions of his Old Guard to stabilise the situation. They attacked without firing, using their bayonets, and after a ferocious fight the Old Guard recaptured the village. The Prussians were still not to be beaten, however, and a final massive Prussian counter-attack evicted the French after some vicious and bloody street fighting. The last to leave was the Old Guard who defended the church and cemetery.

The exact timing of the final expulsion of the French troops from Plancenoit has been a point of argument for the last two centuries. Given that the main road to Genappe stood only 1,100 yards (1,000m) or so away and that all of the evidence shows conclusively that Wellington's troops had passed along this road in immediate pursuit of the fleeing French before the Prussian troops arrived in force on the main road, it is only logical that the final overthrow of the French in Plancenoit had to occur at the same time, or more probably, after Wellington's army had commenced its final and decisive advance after

Prussian medal for the 1815 campaign.

Prussian memorial.

the defeat of the Imperial Guard. Wellington himself was the first to admit that the Prussian attack was vital to the victory in drawing off Napoleon's badly needed reserves. If these had also been available to join the attack against Wellington, it is very doubtful he could have defeated them.

A large memorial was erected in the village to the Prussian soldiers who had died in this contest. In 1832 it was damaged by French troops on their way to Antwerp and since then it has been restored and surrounded by a protective fence.

64 Iron Cross

THE IRON CROSS or Eiserne Kreuz now has con-
notations with the Nazis and the Third Reich, but it
was instituted on 10 March 1813 by the Prussian King
Friedrich Wilhelm III. It was designed by Karl Friedrich
Schinkel, a Prussian sculptor and architect, and was
awarded for bravery in the field, without regard to rank,
during the War of Liberation and the Waterloo campaign.

The order was designated in three levels: Grand
Knight for senior officers only, and the First and Second
Class for all ranks. Most sources indicate that the Iron

**Date of
manufacture:**
1813–15

Location:
Private collection

Cross Second Class was required to be awarded before the First Class but there is some evidence that this was not strictly followed, or that they were issued simultaneously. An even higher decoration, the Star of the Grand Cross of the Iron Cross, was awarded and issued to Field Marshal Gebhard von Blücher in 1813. It has only been issued to one other person – Field Marshal Paul von Hindenburg in 1918. A third award was planned for the most successful German general during the Second World War, but was not made after the defeat of Germany in 1945.

The best figures available indicate that approximately five Grand Crosses of the Iron Cross, 668 Iron Crosses First Class and 16,131 Iron Crosses Second Class were awarded for the period 1813–15; this equates approximately to a rate of one in sixteen men in the army receiving an Iron Cross of some sort.

The 1813 Iron Cross as depicted is made of blackened iron and has a silver edge. The Grand Cross and Second Class hung from a ribbon, but the First Class had a different system of attaching it to a uniform. In this case the obverse had one or two loops welded onto each arm for sewing onto the uniform. It is interesting to note that almost immediately, jeweller's copies were made for the recipients who had lost or damaged their Iron Crosses or who wanted a better-quality version.

The Iron Cross has been reconstituted three times in history and dated with its new inauguration year. These were in 1870, 1914 and of course 1939, when they were issued in huge numbers. In comparison to 1813–15, over 3.5 million Iron Crosses were distributed in the Second World War, giving a soldier a one in five chance of gaining one.

65 Mausoleum of General Duhesme

WHEN THE PRUSSIANS arrived in the vicinity of the Battle of Waterloo, the IV Corps, commanded by General Friedrich Bülow, found itself slightly in the French right rear, beside the straggling village of Plancenoit, which lay in a dip in the land.

It has been claimed that Napoleon was aware of the approach of the Prussians, having observed troops on the march as far away as St Lambert and, having had it confirmed by a captured Prussian hussar that these troops were indeed Prussians and not the French troops under Grouchy, Count Lobau's corps was then sent to counter this attack (see item 36). However, the evidence to support this claim is very questionable. Surveys of the ground between Rosomme and Chapelle St Lambert show that the high ground in between makes it impossible for anyone to have seen anything occurring at that location.

Most witnesses describe the captured Prussian as a 'Black Hussar', but neither of the two hussar regiments that wore black were at Waterloo. It is possible,

Date of construction:
1815

Location:
Ways, near Genappe, Belgium

however, that the captured Prussian was an ex-member of the Life Hussars who had joined the 8th Regiment of von Bülow's IV Corps but still wore his old uniform. The timing of this capture is also very suspicious, as it is stated as happening at 1 p.m., when Bülow was still forming up at Chapelle St Lambert and had not yet sought to proceed further forward.

Tellingly, the memoirs of troops of Lobau's corps are very clear that their initial movement to the right soon after 2 p.m. was actually to shore up the right after the defeat of d'Erlon's attack, to act as a rallying point on which the dispersed troops could form again. They are very clear that the later attack by Bülow's Prussian corps was a complete surprise to them.

The only documentary evidence of the French knowing of their approach at this time is contained in a postscript to a letter from Soult to Grouchy timed at 1 p.m. However, this letter is strangely missing from the Register of the Imperial Staff, which recorded all letters received and despatched. The only copy surfaced in 1818, published by Grouchy as part of his own defence. It is dated from the 'Battle of Waterloo' – a name given to the battle on 19 June by Wellington, a name never used elsewhere that day – and the signature of Soult is particularly questionable when compared with other known examples.

The evidence actually seems to indicate that the Prussians were not seen as they approached and that their attack on Plancenoit was entirely unexpected by the French. Lobau's troops fought bravely but were slowly pushed out of the village. The eight battalions of the Young Guard were sent by Napoleon to retrieve the situation (see item 72). Led by General Guillaume Philibert, first Count Duhesme, they stormed into the village and successfully drove the Prussians back. Around 5 p.m. during the fighting, General Duhesme was struck on the right side of the skull and had difficulty maintaining himself in his saddle. He was taken prisoner as the French army retreated, and he was transported to an inn to be held alongside General Mouton near Genappe. He died of his wounds two days later and was buried at Ways.

66 Casket containing two musket balls

ONE OF THE strangest stories of injuries suffered during the Battle of Waterloo is that of First Lieutenant Thomas Taylor Worsley of the 3rd Battalion of 95th Rifles.

Worsley came from the an old family in Hovingham, Yorkshire. He had served throughout the Peninsular War and was wounded at the siege of Badajoz when a musket ball struck him on the side of his neck. The ball must have struck when it was at low velocity, or 'spent'

Date of construction:
c. 1815

Location:
Private collection

as it was then termed; it only penetrated as far as the muscles, which offered enough resistance to deflect the lead ball in a circuit around the neck and it was finally extracted by a surgeon from the other side of the neck. After this injury Worsley had apparently developed a permanent lean of his head to the right.

Three years later at Waterloo, Worsley was to receive another wound by a musket ball. Amazingly, the wound was a mirror image of the former one, the ball striking the other side of his neck and again making the circuit of his neck before being extracted by the surgeon.

The second injury is recorded to have completely rectified the lean of his head and put it straight again. The two injuries and their effects do sound incredible, but are confirmed by numerous eyewitnesses within the regiment. Worsley retained the two balls that the surgeons had extracted in a little casket.

Worsley left the regiment on half pay in 1816 and in 1848 he received a General Service medal with nine clasps for the battles of the Peninsular War he had served at.

He died in 1851 and was buried at St George's Church at Woodsetts near Rotherham, where there is a plaque.

Such strange tales are not as rare as one would imagine. Lead balls were often deflected wildly in their path within the body and emerged in seemingly unconnected locations. Other examples include a doctors' report of a man shot in the lower thigh, the ball travelling up and around the pelvis only to be extracted from low in the other leg.

67

Coatee of Captain William Miller,
1st Foot Guards

Date of manufacture: c. 1815

Location: National Army Museum, London, UK

THIS 'UNDRESS' OR campaign jacket was worn by Captain William Miller of 1st Foot Guards during the Waterloo campaign. The two battalions of the 1st Foot Guards had suffered severely at Quatre Bras in the fight for Bossu Wood, and Captain Miller died at Brussels on 19 June of wounds he had received there. Whilst still lying wounded near Bossu Wood, he reputedly told his friend Lieutenant Colonel Charles Thomas that he knew he was mortally wounded and that he was pleased that this was his fate and not that of his friend, who had a young wife to care for. He then asked to see the Colours one more time. They were brought and waved round his body; when he smiled and declared himself happy and content he was transported to Brussels. Charles Thomas was unfortunately killed at Waterloo two days later.

At Waterloo the 1st Foot Guards stood on the ridge behind Hougoumont throughout the battle, often formed in squares to fend off the numerous French cavalry attacks. Towards the end of the day they formed line to counter the final attacks of Napoleon's Imperial Guard, but because of the threat of cavalry, they deployed rather unusually four lines deep. As the French Guard advanced across the shallow valley, the 1st Guards lay down to avoid the heavy French cannonade which was designed to soften up their defences.

The initial attack by four battalions of the Middle Guard finally reached the apparently empty ridge line. Here they were suddenly surprised to see the 1st Guards rise from the ground and fire a series of devastating volleys which cut hundreds down in minutes. An attempt by the French to deploy into line from column was prevented by this sudden onslaught; a cheer and a determined bayonet charge caused the French Guard to turn and flee. A second, poorly co-ordinated French attack to the left of the 1st Guards succeeded in pushing back Halkett's British Brigade and Kielmansegge's Hanoverian Brigade, but their advance was stopped by Chasse's Netherland Brigade.

As the 1st Guards pursued the fleeing Frenchmen down the slope, they suddenly became aware that another column of Imperial Guardsmen were approaching and they in their turn were forced to retire rapidly towards the ridge line, where they immediately began to reform their line. While they were still in some confusion, the 52nd Regiment, commanded by Colonel Colborne, launched a flank attack which threw back this third attack and, ably supported by the majority of General Clinton's division, they advanced towards the crumbling French line, as news of the defeat of the Imperial Guard broke the morale of the French army and the cry 'Sauve qui peut' rang out.

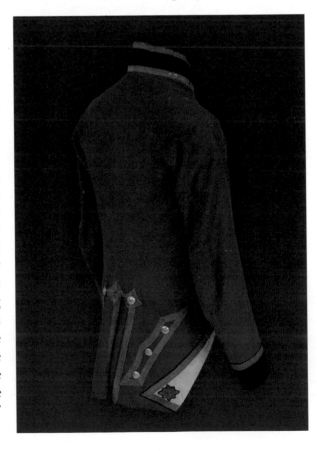

Shaku of the 1st Foot Guards.

Wellington is often criticised for not praising the actions of individual units enough and of praising the Guards too much, his despatch only states 'that the division of Guards ... set an example which was followed by all' – hardly enough to give them all of the laurels of the battle (see item 77). But he has recently been accused by some of carrying out secret communications with Lord Bathurst – for which no actual evidence is produced – by which he gave all of the credit for the defeat of the Imperial Guard solely to the 1st Guards over the claims of the 52nd Foot and others.

What is certain is that when Lord Bathurst stood up in Parliament on 22 June to announce the victory, he did praise the role of the 1st Guards in defeating the Imperial Guard. But who did Bathurst gain this information from? Wellington, in a secret letter? Or a letter from his own son, the Honourable Ensign T. Seymour Bathurst, who just happened to be serving in the 1st Foot Guards?

The Prince Regent announced soon afterwards that the 1st Foot Guards were to be renamed the 'Grenadier' Guards in the mistaken belief that they had defeated the Old Guard, rather than the Middle Guard. As befitted their new status as 'grenadiers', they were issued with a bearskin, replicating largely the headgear of the French Old Guard, which they wear to this day on ceremonial duty.

68

A round of Wellington's tree

DURING THE BATTLE of Waterloo the Duke of Wellington directed most of the battle from a central position near the crossroads above the farmhouse of La Haye Sainte. As he watched the battle from this vantage point, sitting astride his horse Copenhagen, he was sheltered by the canopy of an elm tree. Although Wellington probably never gave the tree a second thought, after the battle it rapidly became an attraction for British tourists who wanted to take home a relic of the battle, especially one closely linked in any way to the all-conquering duke. Soon the tree was relieved of any embedded musket balls, stripped of its foliage, branches and bark and became a sorry specimen. By 1818 the tree was in such a poor state that the local farmer was preparing to cut the remnants down, to prevent further damage to his cornfields from the endless trail of visitors. However, the tree was actually bought by an enterprising Englishman from the farmer and shipped to Britain to be used to produce a number of wooden pieces.

There are wild claims that the tree was bought by a manufacturer in the Midlands to be turned into numerous tiny items, such as tooth picks and snuff boxes, which could be sold at great profit. However, it has been established that it was actually purchased by a Mr John George Children, a librarian in the British Museum,

Date of manufacture:
c. 1882

Location:
Chevening House, Kent, UK

who by mere chance was visiting the battlefield in September 1818 with his daughter and cousin, the day before the tree was to be cut down. A sketch of the elm tree made by his daughter still survives. In spite of his own modest circumstances, he commissioned Thomas Chippendale the Younger, one of London's leading cabinetmakers, to create 'a chair worthy of the occasion', for the Prince Regent. This was presented to King George IV at Carlton House in 1821.

Another chair, with a brass plaque attached claiming its authenticity, came to light recently in Gloucestershire; it went to auction and is now in a private collection. This chair is believed to be one of a pair manufactured in the 1830s with more wood from the tree, with one chair being presented to the Duke of Wellington and the other to the young Queen Victoria. If it is truly one of this pair, it must be the one presented to the queen as the other is known to exist at Apsley House, the London residence of the Duke of Wellington.

Over the years, a large number of other items did appear on the market, claiming to be made from the remaining wood of the tree: a minerals cabinet, work-table, a small stand made by Mr Children himself with the bark still on, to support a bust of the Duke of Wellington. Children disposed of a section of the tree to the Duke of Rutland, a college friend of his, who turned it into a chair too. Beside the three chairs mentioned above, a small table cabinet was sold at auction in 2000 and a writing-table was sold in 2006. It would seem odd that one tree produced such a large number of pieces.

Sir Walter Scott, the poet and avid devotee of Wellington and Waterloo, owned a quaich, or shallow Scottish drinking cup usually with two handles, allegedly made from the wood of the Wellington tree. This was stolen in 1994, along with many other artefacts from Abbotsford House in the Scottish borders, Sir Walter Scott's home. It was recently discovered in a French antique market and has since been returned to its rightful home.

The complete round of the tree illustrated here is kept in the Stanhope family collection at Chevening House. This is now the official country residence of the foreign secretary for the reception of important international dignitaries and so unfortunately this collection is not available to be seen by the general public. It is possible that this was the same piece mentioned above, produced by Mr Children himself as a base for a bust of the duke.

69

The Prince of Orange's horse, Wexy

WILLIAM, THE PRINCE of Orange, commanded the forces of Holland and Belgium (recently amalgamated into one kingdom as the Netherlands) at the Battle of Waterloo. During the final crisis of the battle the prince, riding Wexy, was struck in his left shoulder by a musket ball, and, soon after, poor Wexy was killed by another ball. Opinions are divided regarding the contribution of the prince at Waterloo and British historians rarely give him a good press. Loved and admired by his subjects but despised by the British soldiers, he remains something of an enigma.

William Frederik van Oranje-Nassau was born in 1792 in The Hague, the eldest son of King William I of the Netherlands and Queen Wilhelmine of Prussia. When the prince was only 3, his family had fled to England when the French Revolutionary troops overran Holland. William subsequently spent much of his youth in Berlin at the Prussian court, where he followed a military education and served for some time in the Prussian army. Afterwards he studied at the University of Oxford and entered the British army, serving as an aide-de-camp to the Duke of Wellington, taking part in several campaigns in the Peninsular War. He became one of the close-knit 'family' of Wellington's aides and was nicknamed 'Slender Billy' by the troops.

Date of construction:
1815

Location:
Royal Stables,
The Hague,
Netherlands

215

Representing his father, he returned to the Netherlands in 1813 when the Dutch revolted against French rule. With the help of English and Prussian troops, Holland was freed and his father William regained the throne – rather confusingly also as Prince of Orange.

That year the younger William became commander-in-chief of the joint Netherlands, British and Hanoverian force stationed in the Netherlands. In 1815 when Napoleon escaped from Elba, the forces assembling in Belgium to fight Napoleon grew significantly and the British government sent the Duke of Wellington to take overall command.

Partly to mollify King William, Prince William was given command of 1st Corps, although he was not yet 23. Young and untried as a military commander, William three times ordered troops at Quatre Bras and Waterloo to advance in line rather than square – a very dangerous strategy as it left them vulnerable to cavalry charges and crippling losses. At Waterloo, when the prince insisted that Baron Ompteda, who commanded the 5th King's German Legion Battalion, follow the order to form his battalion in line as they advanced in a bid to retake La Haye Sainte from the French, Ompteda questioned the order. When he was again peremptorily ordered to do his duty, he simply asked to save the lives of his two young nephews, aged 14 and 15, who were with him. Both his nephews did survive, but Ompteda and dozens of his men did not as the French cavalry overran the battalion as predicted.

William received the wound in his left shoulder late in the battle and was taken from the field by his friend and aide Lord March (son of the Duchess of Richmond who gave the famous ball). The prince, dazed, immediately dismounted from his horse and instinctively walked towards the unit which was just in the rear. By now, he had lost quite a lot of blood, had gone pale and needed to support himself against a horse. Eventually he was helped back onto a horse and escorted to the rear by a number of his aides as far as the village of Mont St Jean, where he was placed upon a door and carried to Waterloo village. Here he was treated by surgeon John

Gunning, who reported that the ball had fractured the tip of the scapula and had made a large exit wound.

The prince recovered from his wound and in 1816, at the chapel of the Winter Palace in St Petersburg, he married Grand Duchess Anna Pavlovna of Russia, youngest sister of Tsar Alexander I of Russia, who had arranged the marriage to seal the good relations between Imperial Russia and the Netherlands. However, in 1819, William was blackmailed over his 'shameful and unnatural lusts' – presumably homosexuality.

In 1839, after a revolution, Belgium and Holland became separate kingdoms once more and on his father's abdication in 1840 William acceded to the throne as William II of Holland, which he ruled until his death on 17 March 1849. William enjoyed considerable popularity for his affability and moderation and is generally well regarded in Holland even today.

70

Bearskin of the Imperial Guard

THIS BEARSKIN BELONGED to a soldier of Napoleon's Old Guard, or Vieille Garde, who were the best of the best in his army and bore a fearsome reputation. There were four regiments of the Old Guard, each of two battalions: two of grenadiers and two of chasseurs, although their roles were identical and their uniforms had significant if relatively minor differences.

Traditionally, to serve in the Old Guard you had to be at least 35 years old, have served in the army for a minimum of ten years and to have seen at least three campaigns. It seems that Napoleon hand-picked his Old Guard, selecting only tall men, as their average height appears to have been much greater than those in line regiments.

The Old Guard were not always liked by the rest of the French army. Their privileged pay rates and seniority to the line gave them an air of superiority and allowed them to take whatever they wanted, whilst acting as a 'last reserve' to the army and therefore protected to a great degree from the difficulties that faced a soldier on campaign. They were, however, very well respected, if not feared, by their opponents. Used most often as a final hammer blow against an exhausted foe, they had never been beaten in battle and had secured stunning victories for their emperor on many occasions.

Date of manufacture:
c. 1815

Location:
National Army Museum, London, UK

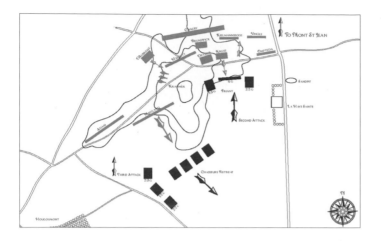

The Old Guard were initially involved in the final acts of the Battle of Ligny, where they drove mercilessly through the town and into the heart of the Prussian position, refusing to take prisoners. This fearsome assault broke the will of the Prussian army, which turned and retreated, but darkness had fallen and this success was not followed up by a vigorous French pursuit (see item 9).

At Waterloo, the Old Guard again remained in reserve until late in the day, when two and a half battalions were ordered to march directly upon Plancenoit to drive back the Prussians, who had finally overcome the efforts of the Young Guard to hold them back. The 1st Battalion 2nd Chasseurs led the charge with Major General Jean-Jacques-Germain Pelet leading them on, the 1st Battalion 2nd Grenadiers and two companies of the 2nd Battalion 1st Grenadiers following up in support. This small force, numbering no more than 1,500 men, marched fearlessly into Plancenoit and with a great roar pushed on through the village, mercilessly bayoneting everything in its path. Such an impetuous attack against horrendous odds should have been doomed to failure, but the Guards' reputation struck fear amongst the Prussians, and the sheer ferocity of their bayonet charges by platoon, supported by the remnants of the Young Guard, caused the Prussians to flee. The Guards charged on through the now burning streets, recapturing the church again and driving the Prussians completely out of the village.

The village was to remain in French hands for the next hour, during which Napoleon launched the remainder of his Imperial Guard against Wellington's army in an attempt to snatch victory from a desperate situation. Severely threatened by the Prussians who again sought to take Plancenoit, Napoleon desperately tried to break through Wellington's now-exhausted defences with one final push. He ordered the remainder of his Guard, supported by both cavalry and artillery, to advance and smash through Wellington's centre.

The 1st Battalion 1st Chasseurs remained to protect his headquarters at Le Caillou, and the 1st and 2nd battalions 1st Grenadiers formed a final reserve near La Belle Alliance. This left only three battalions of the Old Guard for the final push. Modern research shows that the Guard attack partly failed because it was hastily done and therefore made in three uncoordinated waves. The first attack of four battalions of chasseurs was defeated by the British Guards.

The second attack was made to the right of the first and struck Wellington's line at its weakest point and nearly succeeded in breaking through, but was finally driven back by General Chasse's Netherlands Division.

The third attack was made by troops who had initially been left in support, but advanced to aid the Middle Guard; this included the two battalions of 2nd Chasseurs. The attack was defeated by a flank attack led by Sir John Colborne's 52nd Foot and ably supported by most of the 2nd Division, which finally broke the will of the Guard.

The sight of the Imperial Guard retreating, coupled with the realisation that the Prussians had also arrived on their flank, destroyed the fragile morale of the French troops and soon the cry of 'Sauve qui peut' was everywhere.

The two Old Guard grenadier battalions, formed in squares near La Belle Alliance, did become a rallying point and some other units attempted to stem the allied advance, but it was useless, and eventually even these troops attempted to march from the field but then slowly disintegrated.

71 Preserved hoof of Jubilee

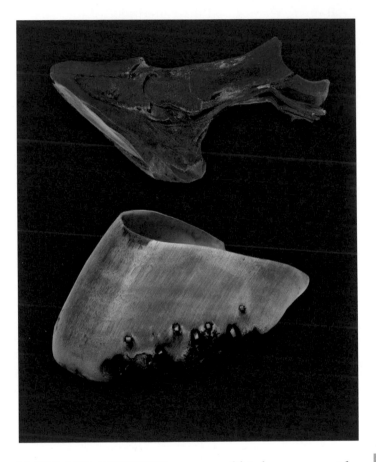

THE BOND BETWEEN a man and his horse cannot be stronger than when a cavalryman is completely reliant on his horse, both as transport, but also often as his saviour in difficult situations. It is therefore not really surprising that many felt a strong affinity with their faithful horses and often sought to keep a memento of them.

Jubilee carried Captain Arthur Shakespear of the 10th Hussars safely through the Battle of Waterloo, and when the horse died some years later, one of his hooves

Date of construction:
c. 1820s

Location:
National Army Museum, London, UK

(opposite page, top) was preserved by his master as a rather gory keepsake.

Retaining a horse's hoof was quite a traditional reminder, as with this one pictured (opposite page, bottom), which belonged to the horse of a trooper in the Life Guards at Waterloo. 'Jock' survived for some twenty years after the battle, dying in 1836. The horse was duly buried in Hyde Park, but the hoof was kept as a memento.

Favourite horses were not an unusual subjects for paintings in a time when rich landowners often also commissioned portraits of their favourite cows, sheep and pigs! This painting reputedly depicts the horse ridden by Captain Frederick Philips of the 15th Hussars at Waterloo. Both horse and master apparently escaped from the battle without a scratch, but it is recorded that Philips had a narrow escape a few days later. On 24 June, during the assault of Cambrai, the 15th Hussars patrolled the suburbs. As Philips was riding through some gardens, the ground gave way suddenly beneath his horse. Luckily Philips was able to extract his feet from the stirrups and propel himself to safety as the horse plummeted all 100 or so feet to the bottom of a hidden well or mine shaft, and was killed instantly. William Dawes of his troop confirms this account in his journal, stating that after cantering through a field of very tall rye, he suddenly lost sight of Captain Philips. On clearing the field, he found Philips standing on the brink of a well. A very lucky escape indeed!

72 Shako plate of the Young Guard

THE YOUNG GUARD was the most junior branch of the Imperial Guard and as such they wore a simple infantry shako rather than the fur busby of the more senior Old Guard and Middle Guard, which consisted of men with a minimum of ten and four years' service respectively. The Young Guard was originally formed in 1809 from conscripts with no prior service, but they

Date of manufacture:
c. 1815

Location:
Private collection

Headwear of a voltigeur of the Young Guard.

were officered by veterans who swiftly turned them into elite troops.

The Young Guard grew rapidly, but was destroyed in the Russian winter of 1812/13. Reformed for the final campaigns in Germany and France in 1813/14, the newly raised regiments of the Young Guard performed very well at the battles of Dresden and Leipzig.

In 1815, sixteen battalions of the Young Guard were formed, but few were ready to go into action when Napoleon ordered his army to invade Belgium: four battalions had been sent to La Vendée to defeat a rebel force and, although the revolt soon collapsed, they were unable to rejoin the army before Waterloo.

Four other battalions served at Waterloo under the command of General Duhesme (see item 65), consisting of two battalions each of the 1st and 3rd Tirailleurs and 1st and 3rd voltigeurs – eight battalions in total. These troops initially stood in reserve in the rear of the French centre, but once the Prussian IV Corps began a serious attack on Plancenoit and started to push Lobau's troops out of the village, Napoleon sent the Young Guard into the village to stem the Prussian advance.

The Young Guard forced its way into Plancenoit and after severe hand-to-hand fighting successfully drove the Prussians back out of the village. However, von Bülow's Prussians were further bolstered by Pirch's troops, who now began to arrive, and the Young Guard were slowly pushed out of Plancenoit in fearsome close-quarter fighting. A counter-attack by elements of the Old Guard stabilised the situation, although General Duhesme was mortally wounded.

Plancenoit was actually held until some time after Napoleon's final attack on the allied ridge had completely failed and the rout had begun in earnest. Seeing the army fleeing in disarray, the Young Guard finally abandoned the village and joined the mass of fugitives.

73

Statue of Cambronne

PIERRE CAMBRONNE (1770–1842) was born in Nantes. He joined the grenadiers as a volunteer at the beginning of the revolution in 1792, serving in Belgium, La Vendée, the Battle of Quiberon, then in the expedition to Ireland in 1796. He was made a colonel at the Battle of Jena in 1806 and was given command of the 3rd Regiment of the Voltigeurs of the Guard in 1810, and was made a baron the same year. Cambronne then fought in Spain and Russia and took part in the battles of Bautzen, Dresden and Leipzig before being promoted to general. He accompanied Napoleon into exile to the island of Elba and returned with him and was made a count by Napoleon when they arrived at Paris.

Of his capture by Colonel Hugh Halkett at Waterloo and subsequent imprisonment in England, there can be no real doubt: for Halkett's story is corroborated by numerous witnesses and is also confirmed by Cambronne himself, who later stated that he had toppled from his horse following a loud explosion near his head, which removed part of his ear and scarred the left side of his head and he subsequently awoke at a British aid station. It is therefore pretty clear that Cambronne was floored by the explosion of a shell and that Halkett did capture him while he was dazed, without any real resistance.

Date of construction:
1848

Location:
Nantes, France

However, a very different version of these events was soon passing around Europe. In perhaps the most poignant description of the Battle of Waterloo, General Pierre Cambronne stood defiantly in the last square of the Old Guard and when urged to surrender, he uttered either the immortal words, '*La Garde meurt, mais ne se rend pas!*' ('The Guard dies, but never surrenders!') or in other versions the rather more succinctly put, '*Merde!*' ('Shit!').

The utterly fabricated last stand of Cambronne and the Old Guard.

However, the whole incident is a fabrication. A French journalist named Rougemont used the phrase in the French newspaper *Journal Général de France* on 24 June 1815 and it soon became known as '*Le mot de Cambronne*'. However, Cambronne was captured a quarter of an hour or more before the French Old Guard squares finally broke up, so he could not have been there. Indeed, he spent the rest of his life denying that he ever said anything of the sort.

After Waterloo, Cambronne was tried for treason, but was acquitted. He later married Mary Osburn, the Scottish nurse who had cared for him while he was wounded.

In 1820, Louis XVIII appointed him commandant at Lille and made him a viscount. He retired to his birthplace of Nantes in 1823, dying there in 1842.

In 1845, the son of General Michel of the Grenadiers of the Guard sought a decree from the king that his father had actually uttered the immortal words before he was killed and provided some evidence from surviving grenadiers. However, the evidence was deemed to be flimsy and the decree was never issued. The phrase could have been spoken by someone else, but it does smack of a grand heroic phrase attributed later by someone seeking to restore some national pride after such a disaster. No witness in either army actually purports to have heard such words that day; it only appears in memoirs written after the events, when the phrase had become synonymous with Waterloo.

Intriguingly, the first time the phrase appears is in the journal of a British officer, one Captain Digby Mackworth, aide-de-camp to Lord Hill, where the exact phrase is used in an entry dated 11 p.m. on 18 June 1815. This could have been added later, although that does not seem to have been the case. So the final irony is that the famous epitaph of the French Imperial Guard could actually have been written by a British officer! But despite all of the evidence to the contrary, the myth of 'Le mot de Cambronne' will probably never fully fade away.

74 Uniform of Private Robert Smith
7th Queen's Own Hussars

IN REALITY THE role of hussars was identical to that of light dragoons; the only significant difference was the often-garish and heavily laced uniforms of the hussars, which tried to emulate the dashing uniforms of the Hungarian hussars formed in the fifteenth century.

Hussars were notoriously impetuous; the great French hussar general, Antoine-Charles-Louis Lasalle, is reported to have said, 'Any hussar who isn't dead by the age of 30 is a blackguard.' The hussars created the tradition of sabrage, the opening of a champagne bottle with a sabre. Moustaches were universally worn; in fact the British hussars were among the few moustachioed troops in the British army, leading at times to their being taunted as being 'foreigners'. French hussars also wore *cadenettes*, braids of hair hanging on either side of the face, until the practice was officially proscribed when shorter hair became universal.

The uniform of hussars included the pelisse, a short fur-edged jacket which was often worn slung over one shoulder in the style of a cape and was fastened with a cord. This garment was extensively adorned with braiding (often gold or silver for officers) and several rows of buttons. The dolman or tunic, which was also heavily decorated in braid, was worn under it. A shako or fur *kolpac* (busby) was worn as headwear. The colours of the dolman, pelisse and breeches varied greatly by regiment, even within the same army, and many garish colours were used, including sky blue, bright yellows and pinks. British hussars also wore the sabretache (a leather pouch hung from the sword belt).

Date of manufacture:
c. 1815

Location:
On display at Brighton Pavilion courtesy of Colchester & Ipswich Museum

Hussars and light dragoons were armed with a curved sabre designed for slashing (see item 15), a short musket or carbine and sometimes also a brace of pistols.

Hussars played a prominent role as light cavalry in the Napoleonic wars. As light cavalrymen mounted on fast horses, they would be used to fight skirmish battles and for scouting. The armies of France, Austria, Prussia and Russia had included hussar regiments since the mid-eighteenth century. In the case of Britain, four light dragoon regiments were converted to hussars in 1806–7, all of which fought at Waterloo.

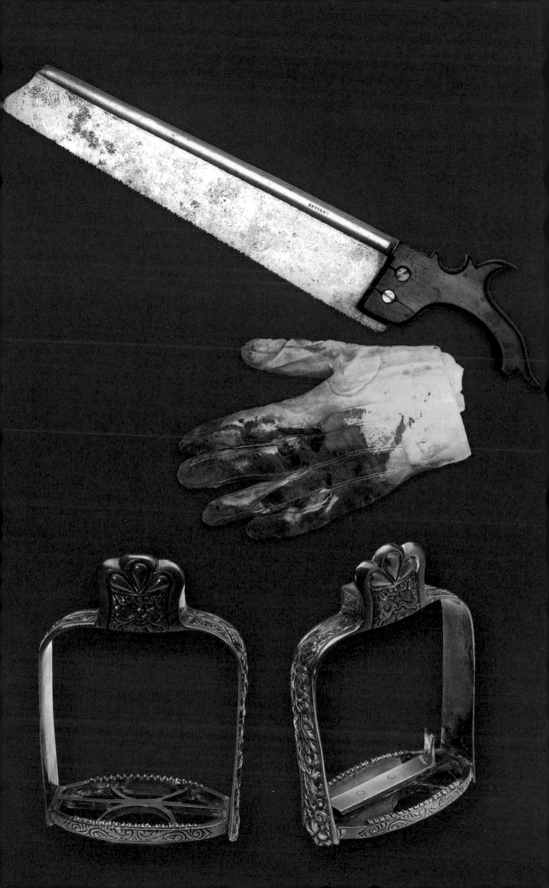

75

Surgeon's amputation saw and bloodied glove

HENRY PAGET, SECOND Earl of Uxbridge, was in command of the allied cavalry and associated Royal Horse Artillery at the Battle of Waterloo. He was a very experienced and talented cavalryman who had shown great promise during General Moore's advance into Spain in 1808 and the subsequent retreat to Corunna.

Unfortunately, the opportunities for such an intelligent senior cavalry officer were curtailed due to family embarrassment. Uxbridge eloped with Charlotte, wife of the Duke of Wellington's brother Henry. The affair ended with Charlotte's divorce from Henry Wellesley and Uxbridge married her in 1810. This affair made it impossible for Uxbridge to be sent to Spain to serve with Wellington.

However, in 1815, Uxbridge was ordered out to Belgium nominally as second-in-command to serve under Wellington. When he asked the duke what his plans were, Wellington reputedly answered, 'Bonaparte has not given me any idea of his projects, and as my plans depend on his, how can you expect me to tell you what mine are?'

Uxbridge was heavily involved in the charge of the British heavy cavalry against d'Erlon's corps, but became too engaged in the attack to ensure that a reserve was maintained, which caused heavy losses

Earl of Uxbridge's stirrups.

Date of manufacture:
1815

Location:
National Army Museum, London, UK

when the French counter-attacked. Later, during the French cavalry attacks against the allied squares, he openly declared that his light cavalry had failed to counter-attack the French with any sort of vigour. However, during the final decisive attack by Wellington's troops, the light cavalry were instrumental in breaking the last vestiges of French defiance.

In the final advance, Wellington and Uxbridge were apparently riding close behind the 52nd Foot when a discharge of grapeshot struck Uxbridge in the leg. This led to the famous exchange: 'By God, sir, I think I've lost my leg,' which received the reply, 'By God, sir, so you have,' which is almost certainly a later invention. Uxbridge had not in fact lost his leg, but his knee had been shattered by the cannon shot and the muscles cut.

Uxbridge was taken to Waterloo village, where deputy inspector of hospitals John Hume, assisted by surgeon James Powell of the Ordnance Medical Department, judged the leg too damaged to save and it was amputated immediately. The glove is one of a pair worn by Uxbridge's aide-de-camp Thomas Wildman, who assisted in the operation. The leg was immediately buried in the garden of the house of Mr Hyacinth Paris and a stone erected over it commemorating the event, stating:

> Here lies the Leg of the illustrious and valiant Earl Uxbridge, Lieutenant-General of His Britannic Majesty, Commander in Chief of the English, Belgian and Dutch cavalry, wounded on the 18 June 1815 at the memorable battle of Waterloo, who, by his heroism, assisted in the triumph of the cause of mankind, gloriously decided by the resounding victory of the said day.

This became a place of pilgrimage and the family made a good living from showing off the stone in the garden and the bloody chair in which the operation had taken place, until 1878, when Uxbridge's son visited and was horrified to discover that the remains of the leg was not buried, but on open display. Apparently the willow

Uxbridge's wooden leg, hat and trousers at Plas Newydd.

tree that had been planted over it had been uprooted during a storm, exposing the remains. This caused a major diplomatic incident, with the Belgian legate in Britain writing home demanding the return of the leg to be buried with Uxbridge. The Paris family refused to hand the leg over without a significant payment to compensate them for the loss of income. The stalemate was only settled when the Belgian Court of Justice ordered the remains to be reburied.

However, on the death of the last Mr Paris in 1934, it is rumoured that his widow, whilst clearing his effects, discovered the leg and papers to prove its authenticity. Horrified at the discovery and not wishing to cause another incident, she burned the remains in her central heating furnace.

Uxbridge – or Marquess of Anglesey as he was then known, having been advanced to this rank on 4 July 1815 in recognition of his services in the Waterloo campaign – used a very sophisticated articulated artificial leg with a hinged knee, ankle and toes, which was invented for him and became known as an 'Anglesey leg'. One of these legs, his hat and trouser leg removed before the operation are still on display at the family home of Plas Newydd on Anglesey. He was affectionately known as 'One Leg' for the remainder of his life.

Anglesey continued his career and eventually became a field marshal, serving twice as Lord Lieutenant of Ireland and twice as Master General of the Ordnance. He died in 1854 and was buried at Lichfield Cathedral.

76 La Belle Alliance

THE ORIGINS FOR the name of this inn are obscure, with many different suggestions about how it was named. Most seem to surround a woman called Barbe Marie Tordeur, who married three times, the third marriage possibly being the great alliance. However, from its inception, the building always included an inn, which expanded over the following years to include a barn and bakery and a drop well.

The property changed hands very regularly but Nicolas Delpierre (a brewer from Plancenoit), bought the buildings on 9 July 1813 and he rented the building to Jean Joseph Dedave, who was proprietor of the inn at the time of the battle. He, like everyone else, fled and hid in the woods to the north when the armies arrived, and the property was pillaged.

The building does not seem to have been used during the battle; it was probably too near the French front line to offer any protection for the French wounded. There is also no evidence that Napoleon or any other great figure ever entered the buildings. The property did receive some damage to the roof by cannonballs, as shown in contemporary prints. Indeed, the building

Date of construction: 1764

Location: Waterloo battlefield, Belgium

simply served as a humble background to fighting and has only gained recognition because of its apt name. It was very near this spot that the Prussian and allied armies first met up in the wake of the fleeing French army, and the name painted on the wall sign must have been remarked on by many.

The momentous meeting of Wellington and Blücher, when they shook hands whilst on horseback and Blücher uttered the immortal phrase, 'Quelle affair', did not happen here but a few miles down the road towards Genappe. However, artists immediately began to picture the meeting in front of the so appropriately named inn and soon a myth was born which has survived the ensuing two centuries.

After the battle, the inn was very popular with visiting tourists and indeed in November 1815 the property was purchased by Richard Ramsay, a rich Scotsman who had lived in Brussels for many years. He soon died and his son, a British army officer named Thomas Ramsay, failed to make the inn a going concern and it was sold to a Belgian family again within two years.

The inn continued to change hands and during the 1830s it became a farm, which it has generally been ever since. Recent attempts to reinvigorate its past as an inn have been mainly unsuccessful. The property has been extensively modified and now bears little resemblance to the inn of 1815.

77

Jacket of Percy,
aide-de-camp to Wellington, and the handkerchief sachet

Date of manufacture:
c. 1815

Location:
Alnwick Castle, Northumbria, UK

THE DUKE OF Wellington began writing his battle report or despatch at Waterloo in the early morning of 19 June and completed it at Brussels later that morning. The despatch is dated 'Waterloo', which is why we know the battle by this name today.

Wellington was renowned for his curt despatches, which many had criticised throughout the Peninsular War. After Waterloo he was exhausted and emotional, yet had to attempt to produce a coherent description of the battle and recommend individuals for their part in the affair, even before any reports from his divisional and corps commanders could be furnished to help him. His despatch from Waterloo was therefore unsurprisingly received quite badly by many. A number of units – in particular the Guards – received fulsome praise, whilst others who expected to receive equal praise, such as the Scots Greys and the 52nd Foot, had no mention at all (see item 67).

Errors were made, including praising a senior Dutch officer who was not even at the battle and stating that three Eagles were being sent to the Prince Regent, when only two had actually been captured (see item 26). But Wellington did give an honest assessment of the Prussian influence on the battle, recording that he would not do justice to Marshal Blücher and the

239

Prussian army if he did not attribute the successful outcome of the day to the timely assistance he received from them.

The despatches written by generals were traditionally carried home by one of their aides-de-camp, who when announcing a victory could expect a reward of promotion to the next rank. For this reason it was a great honour, and on this occasion the duke looked to Major the Honourable Henry Percy of the 14th Light Dragoons to perform the duty.

Percy had been given a purple handkerchief sachet as a keepsake by an unknown admirer at the Duchess of Richmond's ball. When given the despatch, he folded it to fit into the sachet, which was still in his uniform pocket.

Percy left Brussels around midday on 19 June with the two Eagles sticking out of the windows of his carriage. He boarded HMS *Peruvian* of sixteen guns, commanded by Captain White, at Ostend. However, the ship struggled without wind halfway across the Channel and he took to the ship's boat with Captain White and four sailors, each taking an oar, and rowed into Broadstairs, where they arrived at 3 p.m. on 21 June.

A carriage was found and he reached London around 10 p.m. The despatch was addressed to Earl Bathurst, Secretary of State for War, who resided in Downing Street. However, he was not at home, but was dining at Lord Harrowby's at 44 Grosvenor Square.

Percy was also required to present the two Eagles to the Prince Regent, who was attending a ball at Mr and Mrs Boehm's at 16 St James Square. Just as the dancing began, Percy arrived and ran into the house carrying the two Eagles, crying 'Victory, Victory'. The ball ended in uproar, with the prince going into a study to read the despatch and the other guests hurrying away to pass on the incredible news.

Mrs Boehm never forgave Percy for ruining her great moment; in 1819 the Boehms became bankrupt and the house was sold to become the East India Club. Mrs Boehm lived out her life in a grace-and-favour apartment. The prince apparently presented her with a solid gold eagle as a memento of the great occasion.

Percy was made a lieutenant colonel.

78

Waterloo relics

THE DAY AFTER the battle, indeed before all of the wounded had been evacuated to hospitals and the dead buried, the field was drawing crowds. Few stayed long once the reality of the horrific aftermath of such a fierce battle was displayed before them and as they choked on the vile smell of putrefaction that had already set in with the summer heat.

The field had been scoured immediately after the fighting and throughout the night for valuables on the dead and dying, and it is certain that many wounded were finished off by one of these vultures when any attempt was made to resist them. Money and jewellery was the ultimate prize, but weapons and cuirasses were also collected to sell on; bodies were stripped both to aid in the search for valuables and to provide a ready supply of clothing and footwear for the local population. By the following morning, so thorough had their work been that very few bodies had any semblance of clothing remaining on them.

There was still so much detritus from such a battle that for a week or more afterwards visitors could easily pick up a small memento of the fighting. However, the Belgian authorities were not slow to police the field and soon began to search the carriages of the visitors to

Date of production:
c. 1857

Location:
Private collection

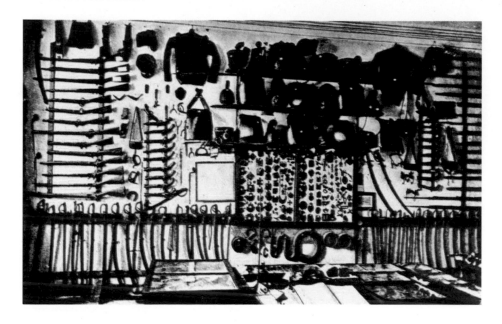

ensure that they were not removing items, and much was confiscated.

As early as 23 August 1815 an advert in the *Morning Post* offered not only to take people on tours to the field of Waterloo but also to see Waterloo relics, and a Mr Peat, a saddler from Piccadilly, already had for sale a cuirass, though he incorrectly stated that it was from a French gendarme slain at Waterloo, as well as a beautiful brass one, again incorrectly stated as being taken from an officer in the Imperial Guard. Both items had been collected from the field of Waterloo by a gentleman who had just arrived from Belgium; they advertised as probably the last to be imported into the country as the Belgian government was now enforcing severe penalties on the removal of any object from the battlefield.

By 17 November 1815 a Mr Palmer had established the Waterloo Museum at No. 97 Pall Mall, at the former Star and Garter Tavern. It was staffed by retired soldiers and men who had lost limbs at Waterloo. The walls of the first room were apparently entirely lined with cuirasses, helmets, swords, guns and bayonets – all picked up on the field of battle.

Monsieur Tussaud's, at 33 Coventry Street, had on display Waterloo cuirasses, swords and Eagles, and

A rare but sadly poor-quality image of Cotton's museum.

apparently a representation of the field of Waterloo the day after the battle was on display at Covent Garden. Mr James Howe commissioned a large mural depicting the Battle of Waterloo where visitors stood in the centre of an oval room and had the battle unfold around them. The mural was based on drawings made by Howe on the spot. It proved incredibly popular and went on a tour of the country.

The most famous panorama was produced by Henry Aston Barker in eight murals that, when joined together, gave a complete 360-degree view of the battle, not unlike the one built by Dumoulin in 1912 on the battlefield itself, which can still be visited today. The Barkers are believed to have made £10,000 from this panorama, which equates to around £450,000 in modern terms.

Troop Sergeant Major Edward Cotton of the 7th Hussars retired from the British army after twenty-one years' service and returned to live at Waterloo, having fought at the battle as a private. Having married a local girl, he set himself up as an innkeeper and battlefield guide and started to collect relics of the battle from the locals who still retained a large amount of paraphernalia. Eventually he built and ran an extensive Waterloo museum, probably the largest collection of Waterloo memorabilia ever.

Cotton died in 1849 and was buried in Hougoumont garden, but was reinterred later as the only non-commissioned man laid in the British memorial at Evere (see item 93). The museum continued until 1909, but tragically it closed and the relics were auctioned in lots and spread across the world.

Rouen Septr. 23d 1815.

Dear Ann,

It was with pleasure I received your kind letter, and am very happy to hear you are in good health as this leaves me at present and in fact I should have wrote you sooner but we have been so very much harassed about of late, and most likely you have heard of the Dreadfull Yet Glorious Battle of Waterloo and perhaps you will like to hear a little of the particulars of our late campaign which I shall endeavour to give you as correct as I possibly can. We marched from Dendahautem in Flanders on the 16th June and marched about 40 Miles that Day but when we had got about 30 Miles we begun to hear the guns rattle pretty quick which caused us to go a little faster but when we had got a few Miles further we Met a great many Wounded Soldiers who informed us they had been engaged but the Frenchmen had got pretty tightly handled and had retired into a Wood so we encamped in an open Field that night and about 4 OClock the next morning we began to put ourselves in readiness and remained in the same position and about 10 OClock we advanced up to the Wood and formed our lines and stayed there some time I suppose about 2 hours when we retreated but it was only to Decoy the enemy from their position and Draw them on to more advantageous situation where we could get fair play at them however they came out and the 7th Hussars attacked them but the French out numbering them so very much they lost a good number and was obliged to retreat but the Life Guards made some very pretty charges on them but the road being so very Muddy the men was almost smothered with Salt and as the 7th Hussars was chiefly attacked in a small village near Genappe that the streets was so very slippery that I really believe they lost more men with the Horses falling and being rode over and at the same time a most Dreadfull Thunder Shower came on with such rapidity that we was completely Wet thro in the course of a few minutes and I continued to wear the Whole of the Night that I can assure you we was in a most Deplorable state by the morning we had not a Dry thread upon us and the Horses were in the same situation for they could not lie down and had not lien down from the 15th Night. B.F.C.

79

Letter from Private Samuel Boulter,
Scots Greys

Date of production:
23 September 1815

Location:
Archive of the Household Cavalry, Windsor, UK

DURING PREVIOUS WARS, letters written home by eyewitnesses were either rare or non-existent; indeed, even during the late wars in Spain and Portugal they still remained a rarity, because of the difficulties of the post and the costs involved.

However, something changed significantly at Waterloo, as the archives of Britain, Europe, indeed the whole world, testify. It would seem that virtually every officer who survived the battle or who escaped with only a minor injury was soon writing home, both to allay the fears of their families, but also to give their version of events, from their limited field of vision in a heavily smoke-laden atmosphere. Officers were almost always guarded in their comments, not wishing to cause offence by criticism and often guilty of embellishing their own role, knowing that what they wrote would often appear in the public domain via the newspapers or at least be discussed within polite society.

A new phenomenon also began to appear: letters from the lower ranks in quite significant numbers. Non-commissioned officers were required to be able to read and write to carry out their administrative duties, and therefore their correspondence might be expected, but it is generally assumed that the simple privates were largely unable to read or write well and

Bruxelles 20th June 1815

My dearest Mama, I wrote to you very lately from hence, yet so eventful, so melancholy & yet so prideful a time has occurred in the short space since then that I can scarcely collect my senses to know what to tell you, the dispatches from the Drake went off yes'y & I wrote a hasty line to Wm. Christian which Shope – went with them in which I requested him to let you know that my Henry was well, either the Gazette or a message from him has I trust given you the comfort therefore of learning that once more my adored Henry's invaluable life has been spared, tho' in hard con= test a battle which has thank God terminated by a most complete victory, & we have reason to think therefore that few of them wrote home with their experiences. But, by the time of Waterloo, this belief is simply wrong: a significant number of letters and journals written by private soldiers have been discovered during the last decade.

The rise in education in Britain, mainly driven by the church schools, was a major influence on this situation and it is estimated that the country had a literacy rate of around 60 per cent in 1815. It is also clear that many adults had had to learn to read and write to aid them in their Bible studies, as the rise of Nonconformism and lay preaching took hold, especially in the army – much to the concern of the Duke of Wellington, who was worried that the egalitarian influence of Nonconformism would lead to a lack of discipline in the ranks. The particular joy of the accounts written by the ordinary rankers is their bold and honest criticisms and usually very modest claims of their own actions – something we also associate with veterans of more recent wars.

Such a plethora of first-hand reports, written before they could be tainted by the accounts of others, is of course of inestimable value to military historians wishing to study the battle. Incredibly over 500 previously unknown eyewitness accounts of the battle have been published in English for the first time in the last decade, which has radically changed our understanding of many aspects of the battle as traditionally told.

It is assumed that there may be many more still to be discovered, kept lovingly within families, and it is hoped that the 200th anniversary will see many of them come to light.

Letter from Susan Clinton, wife of Lieutenant General Sir Henry Clinton, who was at Brussels during the campaign.

8o Bones of the Fallen

AFTER THE BATTLE of Waterloo, the fields were littered with the bodies of both men and horses in huge numbers. Many exaggerated claims still abound, but in reality the bodies of around 12,000 men and 14,000 horses lay across the fields. Thousands more men lost limbs, which were scattered across the landscape. Putrefaction in the hot summer weather soon became a terrible problem and few visiting the battlefield soon after fail to mention the terrible smell of rotting flesh.

In the aftermath of the battle, bodies had been searched for valuables and stripped of any vestige of uniforms, which made identification of individuals, or even their nationality, virtually impossible. Therefore bodies were rarely buried individually or with any ceremony. The vast majority were rapidly heaped into hastily dug trenches, friend and foe together, and covered with a thin layer of soil. For months later, visitors report that the ground was very spongy under foot and in many places a half-decayed hand or foot protruded from the ground, forming a macabre marker.

The bodies of the horses caused an even greater problem as their carcases swelled excessively, making

Date of construction:
1912

Location:
Le Caillou, Belgium

them extremely difficult to move. They were generally dragged with ropes onto large pyres and burned. It is claimed that human remains were sometimes also added to these pyres.

By the early nineteenth century it was widely realised that bones, rich in calcium, were a valuable form of fertiliser, and within a few years of Napoleon's defeat, agents of fertiliser manufacturers were scouring the battlefields of Europe. The bones of men and horses were removed from places such as Austerlitz, Leipzig and Waterloo and shipped, usually to Hull, and then on to bone grinders, many of whom were in the Doncaster area, although some bones travelled as far as Rhode Island in the United States.

This was not a well documented business, but it was reported on and became a part of popular folklore. In 1822, a correspondent wrote in the *Observer* that it was now ascertained beyond a doubt that a dead soldier was a most valuable article, and it was more than likely that the good farmers of Yorkshire were indebted to the bones of their own children for the success of their crops.

In 1912 an ossuary was built in the grounds of Le Caillou to house the bones that constantly surface on the battlefield with each year's ploughing; here they lie intermingled, silent witness to the horror.

81

British Waterloo medal

PRIOR TO THE Battle of Waterloo there had been no official medal produced for the British army for a campaign or battle that was issued to junior officers or the lower ranks. But after Waterloo, an identical campaign medal was produced for all present of whatever rank, for the first time.

Previously, medals had been restricted officially to a gold medal that was issued to the commanding officer of each regiment that actually participated in the battle. The suggestion for a medal issued to all ranks was made by the Duke of Wellington to the Duke of York just ten days after Waterloo; and the Master of the Mint, William Wellesley Pole was soon after commanded to strike two different sized medals in commemoration of the battles of Quatre Bras and Waterloo. Pole immediately wrote to invite artists belonging to the Royal Academy to submit designs for the two medals.

The small medal was initially to be struck in brass, possibly from the captured French cannon, to be issued to every officer and soldier in the British service, including the King's German Legion, who was present at one if not both of the battles. The men were also credited with two years' extra service and pay for pension purposes. In fact, a design for this medal had been formed by the chief engraver of the mint, Mr Wyon, from an

Original medal roll of the Royal Mint, now at The National Archives, Kew, UK

Date of manufacture: 1816–17

Location: Author's collection

ancient Greek coin. The obverse of the medal bears the effigy of the Prince Regent, while the reverse depicts the seated figure of Victory. The ribbon, a thick red band edged in royal blue that mirrored the ribbon used on the previous gold medals, passed through a large iron ring on top. The head of the Prince Regent was taken from a drawing by Sir Thomas Lawrence.

Pistrucci Medal.

The other larger medal, to be struck in gold, was probably intended to be given to each of the sovereigns in the alliance, their ministers and generals. This resulted in the design of the Benedetto Pistrucci Waterloo Medal, which, after a number of design disagreements, took 33 years to complete and was never issued to whom it was intended – the whole idea finally being abandoned in 1849.

Pole made it understood that no other business was to be allowed to interfere with the manufacture of the medals. All the medals would be ready for delivery on 9 November 1815.

What changed and why is uncertain, but on 10 January 1816 Pole wrote a letter to the Lords Commissioners of the Treasury informing them that His Royal Highness the Prince Regent had signified that the medals to the officers and men who served in the Battle of Waterloo should be made of fine silver. He therefore requested the necessary quantity of bullion for this purpose. The weight of the medal was proposed to be 1oz and the number to be struck would amount to 40,000; but to enable the Mint to carry on the work with speed a larger quantity of silver would have to be provided than would ultimately be used – he required 60,000 oz of fine silver for this operation as soon as possible.

By 4 March, Pole could write to Lord Bathurst, Secretary of State for War and the colonies, that the medals were now ready for delivery. He proposed packing the medals in boxes marked on the outside with the corps or regiment to which the medals within belonged; and a copy of the list of recipients was transmitted from the Royal Horse Guards. The medals were supplied fitted with rings, and a quarter of a yard of ribbon. The name of each officer and man was impressed upon the edge of the medal destined for him. There were more than 35,000 names, and he hoped that they would be able to deliver finished medals, packed as mentioned, at the rate of about 1,000 per day. Each medal contained 1oz of fine silver, worth about 6 shillings. There was no difference whatever in the quality, figure or workmanship, between the medals for the officers and those intended for the soldiers. At a cost of 6 shillings each, it would require £120,000 worth of silver to complete 40,000 medals; in modern terms this would equate to over £6 million.

Contrary to the original intention and popular belief, the Waterloo medal was not generally issued to the next of kin of those who were killed in action or who had died from their wounds in the Waterloo campaign. In total the Royal Mint produced 37,638 Waterloo medals.

The medal was not popular in the rest of the British army. The veterans of the Peninsular War felt aggrieved that those who were present at Waterloo – many of them raw recruits, who had never seen a shot fired in anger before – should receive such a public acknowledgement of their achievements while they, who had undergone the privations of the whole war, had had no recognition of their services. Those who still remained alive in 1847 were eventually to gain recognition when Queen Victoria instigated the General Service Medal and allowed veterans of campaigns as far back as 1801 to request a medal retrospectively. Unfortunately, too many veterans had already died feeling disgruntled at their poor treatment.

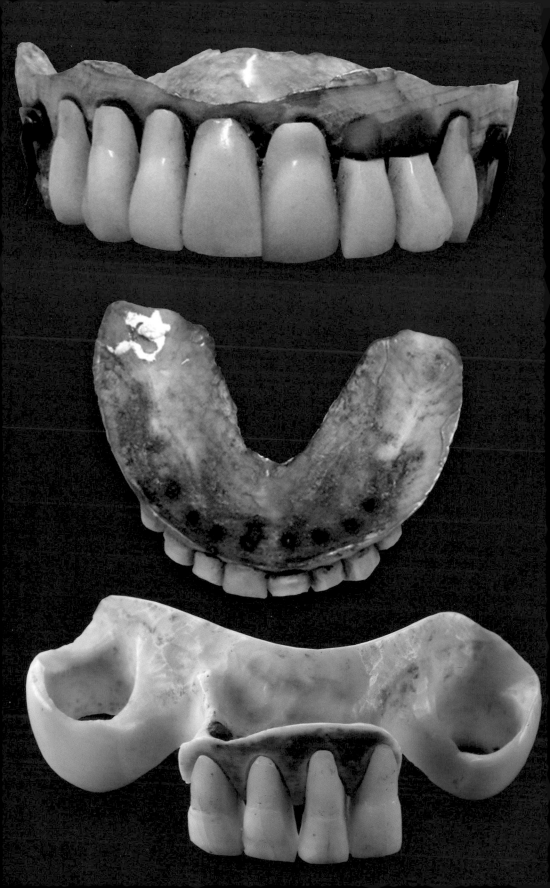

82

Set of Waterloo dentures

AT A TIME when dental health was not really understood and tooth decay was prevalent, there was a constant demand for good-quality dentures. In the late eighteenth and early nineteenth centuries people dreaded losing their teeth: the toothless had sunken cheeks and looked old before their time, and without teeth it was hard to speak intelligibly. In the upper ranks of society, the toothless tended to keep their mouths shut rather than reveal their naked gums. For those who could afford it, the answer was a set of false teeth, but dentures rarely fitted, they looked nothing like the real thing and in most cases were not secure enough to risk eating with. Some early sets of teeth were carved from a single piece of ivory or bone, while in the more sophisticated designs artificial teeth were riveted to a plate made of ox bone or hippo ivory. The biggest drawback of all was that the lack of enamel on bone and ivory meant decay soon set in. The result was inevitable: a rotten taste in the mouth and evil-smelling breath. The fashion for fans was prompted by the all too common need to hide bad teeth and stinking breath. Dentures made from human teeth were much better.

In the early part of the nineteenth century, patients with plenty of money but very few teeth were prepared to pay enormous sums for a good set of dentures, and

Date of manufacture:
c. 1820

Location:
Museum for Health Care, Kingston, Canada

the best had real human teeth at the front. Sometimes the poor could be persuaded to part with good teeth, but people had to be desperate to sell their own teeth. The dead, however, did not need persuading. For the discerning patient, teeth from the battlefield were the best. It was not always what they actually got. Many second-hand teeth came from mortuaries, the dissecting room and the gallows. The biggest purveyors of teeth were the 'resurrectionists' who stole corpses to sell to medical schools; teeth were one of the extra perks of the job. Even if they dug up a body too far gone for the anatomy classroom, they could still pocket a tidy sum by selling the teeth.

Astley Cooper, the most popular surgeon in London in the early nineteenth century, kept a whole band of resurrectionists in business. He bought the bodies, but the teeth went elsewhere. According to his nephew Bransby Cooper, author of *The Life of Astley Cooper*, the bodysnatchers did not always bother to take the body. When graves were disturbed it was not always to obtain possession of the entire body: the teeth alone at this time offered sufficient remuneration for the trouble and risk incurred in such undertakings. Every dentist in London would at this time purchase teeth from these men.

Dentists needed a steady supply of human teeth, and prices were phenomenal. In 1781, Paul Jullion of Gerrard Street in London was charging 2 guineas for a single human tooth. A row of real teeth fetched an astronomical £31 10s. (£2,000 in modern values), and one fellow returned from Waterloo with a box of teeth and jaw-bones valued at £100 (about £3,400 today).

Demand for second-hand incisors usually far outstripped supply, but wars helped make up the shortfall. In the gloom as night fell over the battlefields, after the petty thieves came the final act of desecration: tooth hunters deftly pulled and pocketed any intact front teeth. Tooth hunters followed the armies, moving in as soon as the living had left the field. 'Only let there be a battle and there will be no want of teeth; I'll draw them as fast as the men are knocked down,' says one such hunter in *The Life of Astley Cooper*.

Taking teeth from the dead to replace those lost by the living was therefore nothing new, but after Waterloo the magnitude of it was different – it was done on a truly industrial scale. The fact that these teeth came from dead soldiers did not put clients off: it was seen as a very positive selling point. Better to have teeth from a relatively fit and healthy young man killed by a cannon-ball or sabre than incisors plucked from the jaws of a disease-riddled corpse decaying in the grave or from a hanged man left dangling way too long on the gibbet. Having been plundered from the battlefield, most of these teeth made their way back to Britain, the country best able to afford the new top-quality dentures which would incorporate them.

These then became known as 'Waterloo teeth' and were often worn with a great deal of pride. Worn as something like trophies by elderly dandies, the national-ity of the teeth in question was actually far from certain, and the gullible patriot was as likely to be sporting a countryman's teeth as those of the vanquished foe.

The term 'Waterloo teeth' quickly came to apply to any set of dentures made from young and healthy teeth taken from a Napoleonic battlefield and continued as a term well on into the nineteenth century, becoming less and less historically accurate as time went on. Although wholly artificial teeth began to take over from the 1840s onwards, as late as the 1860s human teeth obtained from the battlefields of the American Civil War were being shipped to Europe for sale.

A · WEEK · AT
WATERLOO
IN · JUNE · 1815

· LADY · DE · LANCEY ·

83

A Week at Waterloo

ONE OF THE great romantic tragedies of the Battle of Waterloo is the story of Colonel William De Lancey and his bride of only three months, Magdalene Hall (see item 14). Clearly in love, the young couple stayed together when De Lancey travelled to join the Staff of the Duke of Wellington as deputy quartermaster general. Unfortunately, De Lancey was mortally wounded by a glancing blow in the back from a cannonball during the battle and then suffered for eleven days before finally succumbing to his injuries.

During that time the devoted Magdalene tended to her husband in a peasant's cottage in the village of Waterloo and later wrote a very detailed journal of their last days together. The handwritten journal was apparently shown to Charles Dickens, who reputedly wept openly when reading it, but it was not actually published until 1906, well after Magdalene's own death. This is a reminder that women were also closely involved with events at Waterloo.

Women camp followers were a normal part of any Napoleonic army; married to a soldier, they either became an unofficial part of the regiment or ran small businesses, providing supplies to the troops at a price. In the French army they became known as *cantinières* or *vivandières*. It could be a very dangerous job – we know

Date of writing:
1816, published in
1906

Location:
Author's collection

that Marie Tête-du-Bois, *cantinière* of the 1st Grenadiers of the Imperial Guards was cut in two by a cannonball at Waterloo.

Other women attended the field to watch over their loved ones during the fighting. The wife of quartermaster Alexander Ross of the 14th Foot remained close to his side during the fighting until told to leave as the battlefield was no place for an officer's wife. Captain Verner of the 7th Hussars also recalls a sergeant major reprimanding his wife for showing fear as she sat on a small pony as the cannonballs flew by; eventually she was ordered to the rear. Jenny Jones of Tal y Llyn in North Wales is also recorded as having stayed with her husband, who served in the 23rd Foot, throughout the battle, and Elske van Aggelin, a women of easy virtue with the Dutch army, also saw out the battle without injury.

Locals occasionally remained with their property – the farmer's wife apparently remained in the attic of Mont St Jean Farm throughout the action in a vain attempt to protect the livestock. The claim of the daughter of Guillaume van Cutsem to have been within Hougoumont for much of the action at the tender age of 5 has, however, been discredited.

Martha Deacon, the wife of Ensign Thomas Deacon of the 73rd Foot was heavily pregnant at the time. She and her children were present at the Battle of Quatre Bras two days before Waterloo and searched the battlefield for her husband that night, having heard that he was wounded. Failing to find him and hearing he had been transported to Brussels, she promptly walked the 20 miles with her young children to find her husband safe there. On 19 June she gave birth to a baby girl who was christened Waterloo Deacon.

The pregnant wife of Private Peter McMullen of the 27th Foot, who was severely wounded at Waterloo, attempted to carry him from the field despite her condition, only to fail when she herself suffered a fractured leg from a musket ball. The pair were safely transported to a hospital in Antwerp and eventually returned to England, where she gave birth to a daughter. Frederick, the Duke of York, stood as godfather to the child, who was named Frederica McMullen Waterloo in his honour.

The day after the battle, Margaret Tolmie, whose husband served in the Scots Greys, searched the field for her husband, who had been reported killed. She was not only lucky enough to identify his body by the initials in his jacket, but also discovered with great joy that he was not actually dead. With the help of two other women, she dragged him to a medical station, where she went into labour and delivered a healthy daughter who was also named Margaret.

However, the most intriguing cases involve evidence that women actually fought in the French army and were killed during the battle. Volunteer Charles Smith of the 95th Rifles apparently found the body of a dead French officer when searching the field the morning after the battle. He was struck by the delicate build and appearance of the corpse and on further investigation he discovered the body was that of a delicate, young and handsome female. Captain Henry Ross Lewin of the 32nd Foot also records that two dead Frenchwomen were discovered in uniform. He reports that he saw one of them dressed in a linen jacket and trousers and that she had been killed by a ball which had passed straight through her head.

84 The Church of St Joseph

THIS CHURCH IN the middle of the straggling village of Waterloo was used after the battle for the collection of the wounded and dying, before they could be transported to hospitals in Brussels and Antwerp.

A small chapel in the Forest of Soignes dedicated to Saint Anne had burned down shortly before this

Date of construction:
1690

Location:
Waterloo, Belgium

church's construction; the inhabitants of Waterloo had wanted to rebuild it but were prevented from doing so by lack of finance. The new Governor General of the then Spanish Netherlands, Don Francisco Antonio de Agurto, Marquis de Gastañaga, intervened to help. The marquis decided that building a new chapel on the site dedicated to Saint Joseph might aid the recovery of King Charles II. The church's architecture, attributed to the Wallonian architect Philippe Delsaux, is in the French Baroque style and was quite out of keeping with the lowly village surrounding it.

With the French Revolution and France's subsequent annexation of Belgium, the royal church was sold as state property. An unscrupulous Parisian businessman named Thomas Gillet bought it at a knock-down price, having already acquired the neighbouring abbeys of Aywiers and Wauthier-Braine. To cash in on his investments, the speculator dismantled the buildings and sold the materials, stripping the lead off the royal chapel's roof to sell to army suppliers to make bullets, but local opposition was so strong that he hesitated to continue. In the meantime Napoleon signed the Concordat of 1801 with the Pope, and the town appealed to their fellow countrymen to buy back the chapel and put it back into religious use, which was successfully achieved by June 1806.

After the battle the church became the obvious place for family and regimental plaques to be put up as a memorial to the fallen and as such became the centre of all commemorations of the battle.

Despite the rotunda and portico being named historic monuments in 1956, the church was in a poor state due to the two world wars, storms and the effects of air pollution. An urgent intervention project was launched on the 150th anniversary of the Battle of Waterloo in 1965, with British help and led by the descendants of soldiers who fought there. During this work the commemorative plaques to the fallen of Waterloo were moved into the main church and unfortunately some are now placed out of public view.

85 Map of the field of Waterloo
by W.B. Craan

AS SOON AS the battle was over, King William of Orange ordered his chief engineer to produce a detailed map of the battlefield. It is particularly significant as the only professional survey of the battle site before the allied ridge was altered significantly in 1824 as work began on the construction of the Lion Mound (see item 95).

Willem Benjamin Craan was born in Batavia in the Dutch East Indies in 1776. His father was a merchant employed by the East India Company. Craan studied at Leiden University, obtaining a doctorate in law in 1795; he married Joanna Frederika Hahn the same year. He was not very interested in the law profession, however, and for the next fifteen years dedicated himself to mathematical studies and music.

Date of production:
1816

Location:
Private collection

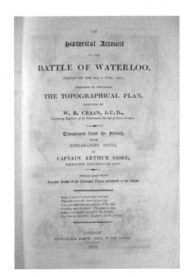

In Aix-la-Chapelle in 1810, he was appointed by the local prefect to the position of surveyor. He performed so well in this function that the next year he was promoted and put in charge of surveying in the department of the Lippe. The collapse of the French Empire in 1814 put him out of work, so he travelled to Brussels, where the future King William I of the Netherlands appointed him as chief of the department of the Dyle. Craan was involved in the project to survey the king's new lands in 1815, when the war prevented any further work.

As the battlefield was close to Brussels, and many wounded of all armies were taken into the city, Craan was able to interview several prominent wounded French and allied officers regarding their experiences during the battle. On the basis of this information, in 1816 he published a detailed map of the battle with an explanatory note, under the title *Plan du champ de bataille de Waterloo, avec notice historique.*

Using the information he had gathered, Craan shows the positions of the various units at Waterloo and also their subsequent movements. The map is slightly unusual in that it has north at the bottom of the map and south at the top – the reverse of standard practice.

The Prince of Orange, who had commanded an army corps at the battle, later viewed the map and approved of it, as did the Duke of Wellington. Emperor Alexander I of Russia was so enamoured of the map that he presented Craan with a precious ring.

For English audiences a book was published in 1817 entitled *An Historical Account of the Battle of Waterloo Intended to Elucidate the Topographical Plan Executed by W.B.Craan, Translated from the French with Explanatory Notes by Captain Arthur Gore, 30th Regiment of Foot.* Gore had actually served at Waterloo.

Craan died in 1848. He was survived by his wife and daughter, Virginie Craan, who was eventually married to Major General Willem Frederik van Bylandt, the commander of a brigade at Waterloo.

86

Napoleon's landau captured after Waterloo

NAPOLEON HAD A number of carriages at Waterloo for use by himself and his Staff. Two of these were captured by Prussian forces in the log jam of vehicles at Genappe as the French army fled: the emperor's personal carriages, one a dormeuse – a carriage with a bed incorporated, and the other a landau – a carriage with two benches set within facing each other, some of which had fold-down canopies.

Coachman Jean Hornn and piqueur or outrider Archambault have left us their memoirs of that night. The emperor's train of baggage remained at Le Caillou until around 8 p.m., when General Fouler, master of the Imperial Stables, ordered them to retire. Archambault apparently locked the dormeuse before it set off – the keys can be seen today at Malmaison, with a label attached stating, 'These six keys belonged to the Emperor Napoleon's carriage, which I was forced to abandon on the road to Quatre Bras on 18 June 1815, the day of the Battle of Waterloo, at eight o' clock in the evening.'

Hornn found the road so congested with vehicles that it took him three hours to get near to Genappe, where he found a complete bottle neck at the narrow bridge over the river Dyle. With the Prussians closing in pursuit, Hornn desperately tried to avoid the jam

Date of construction:
1815

Location:
Malmaison, France

EXHIBITION AT BULLOCKS MUSEUM OF BONEPARTES CARRIAGE TAKEN AT WATERLOO.

by crossing the fields but soon got bogged down in the Belgian mud and he was forced to concede defeat. Being unarmed, Hornn may have expected to be saved, but the Prussian cavalry set upon him, leaving him for dead with ten different wounds. He survived but had to have his arm amputated.

Visitors to Napoleon's coach at the Egyptian Hall, a cartoon.

Major Eugen von Keller of the 15th Infantry Regiment claimed that he had been forced to strike down the coachman to stop the vehicle and that Napoleon had been in the coach at the time, but escaped from one door as von Keller entered by the other. The near-capture of Napoleon would appear to be an invention by von Keller as Napoleon is known to have retreated on horseback and would not have entered the coach when it was jammed and could not move. This is confirmed by men of von Keller's regiment.

This coach had only two seats but was equipped with a writing-desk and a secret compartment: this had held a case containing an unknown but certainly huge haul of jewels and money. It was equipped with two comfortable sleeping compartments, a silver service, a gun rack, a beautifully appointed nécessaire or vanity set given to Napoleon by his wife Marie Louise in 1812, a spirit cabinet, a camp bedstead and bulletproof doors.

In 1824 a number of soldiers from von Keller's battalion took their commander to court in Breslau in an attempt to gain their share of the prize money for capturing the coach and its contents. They were ultimately unsuccessful, but their evidence is invaluable. They stated that as the regiment neared Genappe they encountered the jam of abandoned vehicles and cannon and then saw the carriage in a field, which a number of men approached. Major von Keller then approached and recognised the coach as the emperor's and laid claim to it, promising to share the prize with his men, some of whom he left to recover and protect it. The rest of the battalion continued the pursuit until after midnight, capturing huge amounts of jewels, silver and gold, much of which they abandoned or sold for a fraction of its worth as it was too heavy to carry. During this further pursuit the emperor's landau was discovered near Quatre Bras by Lieutenant Lindenhof of the 15th Regiment.

Von Keller offered the captured landau, which had already been pillaged, to Blücher and retained the untouched dormeuse for himself. Blücher sent the landau to his wife and it remained with his family until 1975, when it was presented to Malmaison Museum.

Von Keller also gave Napoleon's spare bicorn, sword and coat to Blücher, who sent them to the King of Prussia, and they remain on display today in Berlin. He retained the valuables discovered in the carriage, rumoured to be a large quantity of uncut diamonds and some coin, and then sold the coach to a Mr Bullock, who put it on display at the Egyptian Hall in Piccadilly. In 1842 it was purchased by Madame Tussaud's, where it was displayed until it was destroyed by fire in 1925.

DESIGN FOR A MONUMENT
TO COMMEMORATE The Battle of Waterloo, JUNE 18TH 1815.

Dedicated by Permission to His Royal Highness THE DUKE OF YORK K.G.K.B. &c. Field Marshall & Commander in Chief of His Majesty's Forces &c &c &c
by His Royal Highness most obedient & devoted
Humble Servant

87

Proposed design for a monument
to commemorate the Battle of Waterloo

FOLLOWING THE BATTLE of Waterloo, there was great public clamour to erect a memorial to the famous victory, and designs were requested for something to rival Nelson's Column. However, the project never came to fruition due to lack of finances.

A new bridge that was already under construction over the Thames was eventually opened in 1817, named Waterloo Bridge. This bridge became unsafe in the 1920s and a replacement was completed by 1945.

Wellington Arch was originally designed, along with Marble Arch, to form grand entrance gates to the newly built Buckingham Palace, but both have since been relocated. The Wellington Arch, designed in 1828 by Decimus Burton, a leading architect of the day, is a masterpiece of neo-classical design. It was erected as the main western entrance to St James's Park and the Green Park.

Ten years later, following the unveiling of a fine equestrian statue of King George III by Matthew Wyatt in Cockspur Street, a proposal was made to erect an equestrian statue of the Duke of Wellington in the West End of London. A General Committee for the 'Wellington Military Memorial' was formed under the chairmanship of the Duke of Rutland, but Decimus Burton objected strongly to the proposal – his plan was to top the arch

Design only:
1815

Location:
London, UK

273

with a figure in a four-horse chariot and he considered that an equestrian statue would be both out of place and out of proportion.

By July 1839 subscriptions for the statue had reached £14,000 (around £700,000 in modern terms). In 1846 the arch was finally crowned by Matthew Cotes Wyatt's giant equestrian statue of the Duke of Wellington. Thirty men were engaged in the work, which took over three years. Wellington sat for the sculptor and is depicted wearing his customary short cloak, mounted on his favourite charger Copenhagen. The statue is chiefly made of bronze from cannon captured by the British at the Battle of Waterloo.

The Wellington Arch
circa 1870.

To move the statue from Wyatt's studio in the Harrow Road to Hyde Park Corner, the roof of the foundry was removed. The statue was hoisted by blocks and tackle and placed onto a specially constructed enormous wooden carriage weighing 20 tons and with wheels 10ft in diameter.

But by 1882 traffic congestion around Hyde Park Corner had become so intense that a proposal was made to demolish the arch to allow the road to be widened. Public sentiment was opposed to such destruction and the arch was moved to its present position opposite Apsley House. The statue, however, was left abandoned in a corner of Green Park for a year while various possible sites were considered, including Chelsea Hospital, Horseguards, Portsmouth, Wellington College and St James's Park. These were all rejected and in the end a resolution of both Houses of Parliament gave permission for it to be moved to Aldershot.

Pickford and Co. were given the task of moving the statue to Aldershot and this was accomplished in four days during August 1884 using a 12ft-wide trolley drawn by sixteen horses. In 1885 the giant statue was erected on a small knoll called Round Hill near the Royal Garrison Church at Aldershot. Only by standing beneath the statue can one appreciate its colossal size. It is nearly 30ft high, 26ft from nose to tail, over 22ft in girth and weighs 40 tons.

The Wellington Arch has been crowned since 1912 with Adrian Jones' quadriga, which echoes Decimus Burton's original concept.

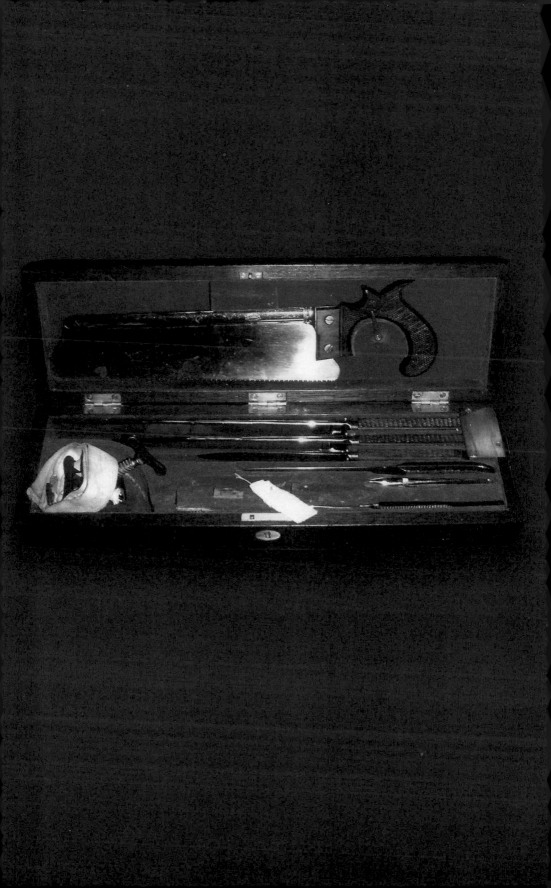

88

Surgeon's amputation set

THE MASSIVE NUMBER of casualties from the battles of Quatre Bras, Ligny and Waterloo simply overwhelmed the medical services of the army. With the wounded numbering in excess of 40,000, there were shortages of ambulances, adequate surgeons, hospitals and medical supplies to cope with these numbers.

There was a huge shortage of stretcher bearers, leading to masses of the wounded having to lie out on the battlefield overnight. Many of these poor unfortunates, without basic medical attention, either slowly bled to death, succumbed to the chill night air or fell to the blade of the avaricious scavengers as they looted the field.

Those fortunate to survive that dreadful night had a reasonable chance of being collected by a party from their regiment, ordered to succour their wounded – and were laid next to the road to await transport to the hospitals. But those who had fallen in obscure areas away from the regiment were likely to be missed and certainly no one initially came for the French.

The Belgian authorities immediately stepped in to prevent a human tragedy. The mayor of Brussels ordered every horse and carriage in the city to be sent to the battlefield to collect the wounded and transport them to Brussels; every household was expected to take

Date of manufacture:
c. 1815

Location:
Private collection

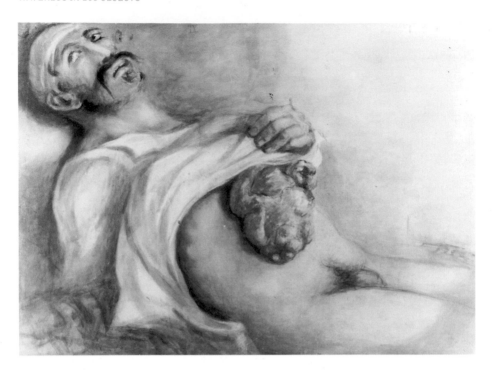

in a number of the wounded and to care for them, and every surgeon was required to attend the hospitals and carry out visits to those dispersed in private properties. Six major buildings in the city were rapidly turned into makeshift hospitals and dozens of smaller ones added as numbers continued to flood in. Genteel ladies were seen tending the wounded, ripping muslin dresses into strips for bandages, providing food and water and comfort; everyone, it seems, played their part. Despite all of these efforts, it is recorded that some wounded lay on the battlefield for up to four full days before they were recovered. As Brussels filled to bursting, more were shipped on to Antwerp, where further hospitals were formed.

Bell's drawing of soldier Peltier wounded in the abdomen by a sword, the colon protruding, 2 July 1815.

News of the battle had reached Britain with great speed; the joy and celebration were clear to see, but many also mourned their losses and the situation occasioned a unique response. Numerous eminent surgeons packed their medical bags and took the packet for Belgium, immediately setting their hand to surgery and tending to the most complicated cases. Amongst these was Sir Charles Bell, who performed a number of amputations but was criticised by some of his peers for his poor success rate; he also produced a wonderful series of sketches of his patients, recording their names, regiments, wounds, treatment and prognosis. In many instances, even after he had returned to London, he maintained a correspondence with fellow surgeons in Brussels to discuss these cases and their outcomes.

Despite all of the problems, hospital survival rates were quite remarkable, with only 9 per cent of admissions succumbing to their wounds or subsequent complications. Indeed, within a year, it was recorded that around 77 per cent had returned to military duties either with their regiment or a veteran battalion. The great majority of the remainder had been discharged and few stayed in the hospitals.

The survivors who were too badly maimed to remain in the army were the real unfortunates in this situation. Discharged from the service by a medical board, they were sent home with a pittance of a pension, which they could barely live on. Unable to work and with little income, many Waterloo heroes saw out their last few years in penury and died in workhouses or simply as beggars on the streets.

VICTOR HUGO

LES

MISÉRABLES

II

PREMIÈRE PARTIE

FANTINE

II

J. HETZEL
LIBRAIRE-ÉDITEUR
18, RUE JACOB, 18

PARIS

89

Victor Hugo's *Les Misérables*

VICTOR HUGO BEGAN writing his mammoth novel *Les Misérables* in 1846 and it was finally published in five volumes in 1862.

In his preface Hugo states that the purpose of his book was to highlight that

> So long as there shall exist, by reason of law and custom, a social condemnation, which, in the face of civilization, artificially creates hells on earth ... the degradation of man by poverty, the ruin of women by starvation, and the dwarfing of child hood by physical and spiritual night ... so long as ignorance and misery remain on earth, books like this cannot be useless.

In its original form the book numbers some 2,783 pages, of which nearly 1,000 digress from the novel on a multitude of essays on random subjects. At the beginning of Volume II, entitled *Colette*, Hugo devotes nineteen chapters to the Battle of Waterloo; he visited the battlefield in 1861 and he completed the book there.

He gives us a vivid and extensive account of the Battle of Waterloo which marks the defeat of Napoleon and the end of any hopes of reviving his empire. Hugo states that most accounts of the battle were told from the

Date of printing:
1862

Location:
Private collection

281

viewpoint of the victorious British, and he resolved to focus his account on the efforts of the French forces. In his version Napoleon is viewed in great awe by his soldiers, but despite his military brilliance they are defeated by the weather. Hugo claims, however, that the real victors of Waterloo are the individual men who are standing up for their rights and beliefs.

The 'Wounded Eagle' monument dedicated to the last combatants of the Grand Army.

During the description of the battle, Victor Hugo embellished a number of scenes with a novelist's touch. He records that the delays in forming up the French artillery because of the mud allowed the Prussians time to arrive; he describes the fierce fighting at Hougoumont and claims that the French were massacred in the chapel, others broke into the formal garden and that the well was heartlessly filled with the bodies of both dead and wounded Frenchmen; that only forty-two defenders survived from La Haye Sainte; that the French cavalry was destroyed plunging into a hidden chasm behind the allied ridge line but still broke seven squares and took six Colours; that Cambronne died refusing to surrender, having replied, 'Merde' to British appeals for the Guard to surrender and that Wellington later said, 'They have changed my battlefield.'

Over time, the novel's descriptions of events have come to be taken as established fact and have distorted the telling of the true story of the battle. Recent investigative work within the primary source material in the archives and forensic archaeology on the battlefield have proven Hugo's version to be factually incorrect and purely based on myths.

Hugo was also aware of the English and German memorials at the site, pointing out that there was no French memorial at Waterloo. He was an instigator of the 'Wounded Eagle' memorial, although it was erected in 1904, well after his death.

Hugo reconciled the defeat of the French army with the idea that it was a victory for civilisation. He was of the opinion that Napoleon's defeat was pre-ordained because the tide of history required his removal from the stage He went on to say that Waterloo represented the revenge of counter-revolutionary forces, but that changes in the political landscape prevented them from reasserting themselves completely afterwards, creating a post-war Europe with greater liberty than before, even under the old leaderships.

90

Model of the Battle of Waterloo

LIEUTENANT WILLIAM SIBORNE of the 47th Foot was an expert in topography and its use in military operations, publishing two works on the subject of the use of landscape models to illustrate them in 1822 and 1827. He was appointed assistant military secretary to the Staff of the commander-in-chief in Ireland and retained this post under four successive commanders. In 1830 General Lord Hill, commander-in-chief of the army, offered financial support to Siborne to produce a topographical model of the battlefield of Waterloo.

Siborne was granted extended leave and he lived at La Haye Sainte farmhouse for eight months whilst surveying the fields and interviewing farmers regarding the crops grown at the time. Unfortunately, Siborne had been given this commission a bit too late, as the Lion Mound had been constructed four years earlier, markedly altering the landscape of the allied ridge (see item 95). This forced him to estimate the appearance of this portion of the battlefield.

During this period of reflection, Siborne developed the idea of adding troops to the topographical model, representing a particular moment of the battle. Lord Hill approved the idea. The model would illustrate the position of all the troops at 7.45 p.m., when the British troops finally faced the Imperial Guard.

Date of construction:
1838

Location:
National Army Museum, London, UK

To ensure great accuracy in the position and formation of the various armies, William Siborne sent out a circular letter to every surviving British and King's German Legion officer to request their memories of the situation at this time and the crops around them.

Despite a change of government and subsequent removal of funding, Siborne took the brave, although ultimately costly, decision to take out loans to complete the project. The model was built in Ireland in thirty-nine sections for £3,000 (about £140,000 in modern terms) with thousands of model figures produced to illustrate it. It was shipped to England and put on display at the Egyptian Hall in Piccadilly in 1838. The model measures 27ft 8in (8.5m) by 19ft 8in (6.0m) and represents the battlefield at the scale of 1:100. One hundred thousand visitors paid 1 shilling each to view the model, but Siborne's financial incapacity meant that he still failed to make a profit from the venture.

Despite this financial disaster, Siborne looked to turn his fortunes around by producing another model. This second, larger model depicts the charge of the British heavy cavalry at 2 p.m. and this survives today at the Royal Armoury in Leeds.

William Siborne finally achieved success in 1844 with the publication of a *History of the War in France and Belgium in 1815* in two volumes. This utilised all of his correspondence with hundreds of surviving officers to construct the first in-depth history of the battle. For more than a century his history stood proud, but Siborne never served in the higher echelons of the army and was not an expert in military matters. Modern historians acknowledge his efforts to gain first-hand evidence from eyewitnesses, but question many of his conclusions and today his history is seen as outdated.

However, some have sought to twist Siborne's difficult relationships with the Treasury and senior military and political figures into evidence of a conspiracy to prevent his model from supporting the Prussian claim to have brought victory to a virtually defeated Wellington. The identity of the author of these conspiracies has tended to point to the Duke of Wellington, who it is claimed, destroyed Siborne to save his own reputation. The evidence, however, is flimsy and often contrived; in fact there really is no hard evidence to prove any form of conspiracy – but as with all conspiracy theories innuendo is enough to keep the convinced believing.

The model was bought by subscription after Siborne's death and placed in the United Services Museum and after a number of further moves has now found a permanent home at the National Army Museum.

Siborne's son published a large number of the letters sent to his father as the *Waterloo Letters*; these have formed an important source of information for historians of the battle ever since. The remainder of his invaluable correspondence with eyewitnesses from the Battle of Waterloo was published by the author in 2004.

SURRENDERED TO H. B. M. S. BELLEROPHON CAPT MAITLAND.

BRENET F.   XV. JULY   MUDIE F.
                   MDCCCXV.

91

Medallion
commemorating the surrender of the Emperor Napoleon by Mudie

Date of manufacture: 1820

Location: Private collection

THE FINAL ACT of the Waterloo campaign was the surrender of Napoleon to Captain Maitland onboard HMS *Bellerophon* at Rochefort on 15 July 1815, just four weeks after his defeat at Waterloo. The medal illustrated is one of a series from 'The Grande Series of National Medals', produced by James Mudie in 1820; there were forty medals in all.

HMS *Bellerophon* was a 74-gun, third rate ship of the line of the Royal Navy. Launched in 1786, she had served throughout the Napoleonic wars, mostly on blockades or on convoy duties. Known colloquially to sailors as the 'Billy Ruffian', she fought in three major fleet actions, the Glorious First of June, the Battle of the Nile and the Battle of Trafalgar. In 1815 *Bellerophon* was assigned the blockade of the French port of Rochefort on the Atlantic coast. Royal Navy ships were sent to watch Rochefort because as early as 9 May 1815 General Henry Clinton, commanding the 2nd British Division at Waterloo, wrote home to his brother with information relating to Napoleon's escape plan if his great gamble failed. Clinton requested that his brother (General William Clinton) inform the Admiralty immediately that two frigates were lying at Rochefort, fully provisioned in readiness to carry Napoleon to America. This information turned out to be correct in every detail.

After his defeat at Waterloo and the realisation of the impossibility of continuing the war, Napoleon attempted to flee to the United States. The two ships were already prepared and waiting for him at Rochefort, but finding escape to America barred by the blockading *Bellerophon*, Napoleon sought other means of escape. Various plans were suggested, including one of hiding the emperor and his followers in casks on an American merchant vessel, but ultimately the ignominy of being caught in such an inglorious fashion led Napoleon finally to come aboard *Bellerophon* to surrender to the British. Napoleon was being pressured to leave French soil by the interim French government in Paris. If he delayed, he risked becoming a prisoner of the Bourbons or the Prussians, who would probably have had him hanged as the enemy of all Europe. Napoleon hoped that the British government would allow him to see out his days living as a private individual in England.

Napoleon embarked aboard the French brig *Épervier* early in the morning of 15 July, and made his way towards the *Bellerophon*. As he approached, the 74-gun *Superb*, flying Vice Admiral Hotham's flag, was sighted approaching. Concerned that the brig might not reach *Bellerophon* before the *Superb* arrived, and that consequently Hotham would take over and receive Napoleon himself, Maitland sent *Bellerophon*'s barge to collect the former emperor and transfer him to the ship. Around 7 a.m., the barge pulled alongside *Bellerophon* and Napoleon and his entourage climbed aboard. Napoleon walked to the quarterdeck, took his hat off to Maitland and in French announced, 'I am come to throw myself on the protection of your Prince and your laws.'

Maitland placed the great cabin at Napoleon's disposal, and gave him a tour of his ship. Admiral Hotham came aboard himself to meet the former emperor, and a grand dinner was held in the great cabin. The following day Napoleon visited Hotham on the *Superb*. On his return, Maitland began the voyage to England in company with HMS *Myrmidon*.

Bellerophon anchored off Brixham on the morning of 24 July, and there Maitland received orders from

Napoleon drawn by Planat onboard HMS *Bellerophon*.

Admiral Lord Keith to 'prevent every person whatever from coming on board the ship you command, except the officers and men who compose her crew'. However, word eventually leaked out that Napoleon was onboard the ship and the news created a sensation, with large numbers of boats filled with sightseers soon surrounding the ship and occasionally Napoleon would come out to look at them.

Bellerophon spent two weeks in Plymouth harbour while the authorities came to a decision about what to do with Napoleon. On 31 July they communicated their decision to Napoleon that he was to be exiled on the remote island of St Helena. However, *Bellerophon* was not to take him into exile. The Admiralty was concerned that the ageing ship was unsuitable for the long voyage to the South Atlantic, and the 74-gun HMS *Northumberland* was selected for the task.

On 7 August Napoleon thanked Maitland and his crew for their kindness and hospitality, and left the *Bellerophon* where he had spent over three weeks without ever landing in England, transferring to HMS *Northumberland*, which promptly sailed for St Helena.

Never inclined towards sentimentality, the Admiralty saw no future use for the tired old ship; it proved to be *Bellerophon*'s last seagoing service. She sailed immediately to Sheerness, where she was paid off and converted into a prison ship and renamed *Captivity* in 1824. Moved to Plymouth in 1826, she continued in service until 1834, when the last convicts held onboard left. The Admiralty ordered her to be sold in 1836, and she was broken up. A sad end for an illustrious ship.

92 Waterloo Fund collection box

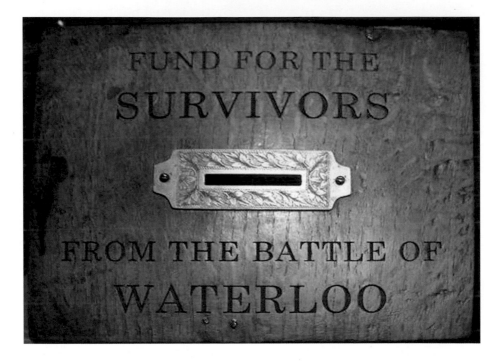

AMIDST ALL THE rejoicing, thoughts soon turned toward the dead and wounded of the battle. A 'Great Patriotic Meeting' was held in London at the City of London Tavern of merchants, bankers and others to consider opening a subscription for the relief of the wounded and the widows of those who fell in the Battle of Waterloo. The committee was to be known as the City Committee. The chair was taken by the banker Alexander Baring – of the Barings Bank which collapsed so spectacularly in 1995. As the government would do little for these unfortunates, it fell to private benevolence to provide such aid. The meeting ended with £500 having been subscribed.

Date of manufacture:
1815

Location:
Private collection

Waterloo Subscription
28th June 1815
City of London Tavern
15th September 1815

Regulations
All Applications must be made by Letter, addressed to the Committee, at the City of London Tavern. Personal application is not required, and cannot be attended to.

the Widows
Widows & dependent
Relatives of officers
killed,

] are requested to state
] their cases, and
] the number and
] ages of their children,
] in a letter addressed
] to the committee; and to
] produce a Marriage
] certificate: or their
] circumstances and
] may be made known and
] recommended to the
] committee by any
] respectable person,
] accompanied
] with similar documents.

Widows & dependent
Relatives Of Non-Commissioned
Officers And Private soldiers killed,

] are required to be
] recommended by the
] Minister of the Parish, or
] the Chief Magistrate of
] the place in which they
] dwell. Widows must send
] to the Committee a
] Certificate of Marriage,
] and also a Certificate
] of the number, and ages
] of their children. Relief will
] be afforded to Widows
] when they arrive at their
] fixed place of settlement:
] the Relief will be placed in

] the care of the Minister
] of the Parish, or of some
] respectable person, to
] be given in such portions
] and at such times as may
] be most useful and
] beneficial to them.

Non-Commissioned Officers and
Private Soldiers wounded,

] are required to have
] passed the examination
] of the Board at Chelsea,
] and to have received a
] Ticket of
] recommendation from the
] examining Officer and
] Surgeon. They will not be
] assisted in London,
] unless it be their fixed
] place of abode; but they
] will receive the relief
] from the Minister of the
] Parish, or from the Chief
] Magistrate of the place of
] their dwelling,
] at such times and in such
] portions as may be most
] useful and beneficial to
] them.

Orphan Children of Officers,

] It is requested that the
] cases of orphan children
] may be stated by their
] relatives or friends, in a
] letter addressed to the
] Committee.

The Committee will be ready to give immediate relief to such Sufferers
of the British Army, engaged at Waterloo, as are now on the Continent,
and may stand in need of such an assistance.

But this was not the end of it: in Edinburgh a similar subscription was opened, headed by the poet Sir Walter Scott. A separate meeting of the 'Noblemen and Gentry' of London was held on 11 July at the Thatched House Tavern, St James, chaired by the Duke of York, to organise a subscription for the widows and orphans of Waterloo; this was to be known as the Westminster Committee. Amongst those present was William Wilberforce, MP, and the Bishop of London. The subscription had originally been for British soldiers only, but Mr Wilberforce suggested that Hanoverians, Belgians, the King's German Legion and the Prussians should be included and sums were sent to these countries for distribution.

The appeal captured the public imagination as nothing had previously; the officers and men of many regiments voted a day's pay to go to the relief of the widows and orphans of the battle; theatres and musicians gave away the profits of a night's performance. Large collections were made across the country, and indeed the empire, with India producing a very large sum indeed.

By June 1820, the fund had received over £600,000 (about £23 million in modern terms), and this was distributed with commendable speed. Widows were granted life annuities, children annuities up to the age of 14 and an additional payment on marriage; allowances were also made to orphans and disabled soldiers (officers and men) received life annuities.

All of this care and compassion was looked upon with great bitterness by one group of people. Little had been done for those who had suffered similarly throughout the wars against Revolutionary and Napoleonic France. Scottish Widows had been formed in 1812 as a fund for securing provisions to widows, sisters and other female relatives of fundholders so that they would not be plunged into poverty on the death of the fundholder during the Napoleonic wars or beyond. But this was the birth of life assurance, not a general fund to relieve those who suffered. Too many Peninsular War veterans died in abject poverty, shamelessly ignored by their ungrateful country.

93 Waterloo Memorial

IN A CORNER of Brussels Cemetery in Evere, just behind the NATO buildings, lies a near-forgotten British memorial. It is dedicated to the officers and soldiers of Britain who gave their lives in the Battle of Waterloo and were buried in Belgian soil. The idea of bringing together

the remains of the British soldiers who had been killed during the Waterloo campaign was first suggested in 1861. In 1882, the Council of Brussels approved a suggestion to donate 30m² (36 square yards) of the cemetery to rebury British soldiers whose graves lay in Brussels or near the battlefields of Waterloo and Quatre Bras. In 1888, a public subscription was launched by Queen Victoria to finance a suitable monument. The sculpture, by Jacques de Lalaing, is a large set of bronze figures depicting Britannia with lowered trident, surrounded by discarded equipment and recumbent lions; on the sides of the base are attached shields bearing the names of the regiments who fought in the campaign. The monument was unveiled by the Duke of Cambridge, commander-in-chief of the British Army, in 1890.

Below the monument is a crypt containing seventeen bodies, which were brought here between 1890 and 1894 from their various burial sites at the battlefield or various cemeteries in Waterloo and Brussels. The only non-commissioned officer buried here, is Sergeant Major Edward Cotton of the 7th Hussars, who survived the battle to become a guide to the battlefield, curator

Date of construction:
1890

Location:
Evere Cemetery, Brussels, Belgium

Engraved tablets within the crypt.

of a museum of artefacts and author of an early history of the battle (see item 78). He was originally buried in the walled garden of Hougoumont after his death in 1849, alongside Captain Lucie Blackman who had died there during the battle.

There is no mention of this hugely important memorial at the battlefield site near Waterloo, and many visitors do not even know it is there. Every year in June the Royal British Legion holds a wreath-laying ceremony for the officers and soldiers who died in the Waterloo campaign. In recent years more and more people are starting to visit the monument thanks to the legion's efforts to heighten people's awareness of its existence.

The bodies re-interred here are:

Colonel Sir William de Lancey, deputy quartermaster general

Lieutenant Colonel the Hon. Sir Alexander Gordon, aide-de-camp to the Duke of Wellington

Lieutenant Colonel Edward Stables, 1st Foot Guards

Lieutenant Colonel William Milnes, 1st Foot Guards

Major William Lloyd, Royal Artillery

Major Archibald Maclaine, 73rd Foot

Captain Edward Grose, 1st Foot Guards

Captain Thomas Brown, 1st Foot Guards

Captain John Blackman, Coldstream Guards

Captain William Stothert, 3rd Foot Guards

Captain the Hon. Hastings Forbes, 3rd Foot Guards

Lieutenant Michael Cromie, Royal Artillery

Lieutenant Charles Spearman, Royal Artillery

Lieutenant John Clyde, 23rd Welsh Fusiliers

Ensign James Lord Hay, 1st Foot Guards, aide-de-camp

Ensign the Hon. Samuel Barrington, 1st Foot Guards

Sergeant Major Edward Cotton, 7th Hussars.

94 Southey's *The Poet's Pilgrimage to Waterloo*

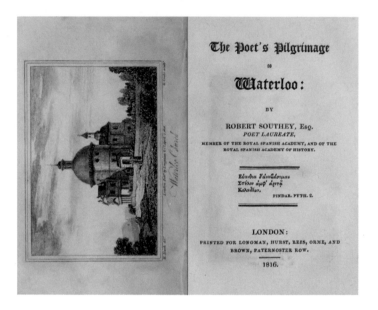

THE DRAMATIC FINALITY of Waterloo inspired a generation of poets and writers to pen their thoughts on the subject. Indeed, anyone with a literary bent appears to have been enthused to write. These works were often very lengthy and turgid, but a few possess some merit.

George Walker had published a poem entitled 'The Battle of Waterloo' before the year was out, as did Sir Walter Scott with 'The Field of Waterloo', and he followed this up with 'Paul's Letters to his Kinsfolk'.

The following year Robert Southey the Poet Laureate wrote a long poem of his visit to the battlefield entitled *The Poet's Pilgrimage to Waterloo*; Lord Byron wrote of the battle in his *Childe Harold* and in 'The Eve of Waterloo'.

Date of printing:
1816

Location:
Private collection

Part of Lord Byron's collection from the battlefield of Waterloo.

Thomas Hardy wrote a poem entitled 'The Field of Waterloo'; William Thackeray also included the battle in his novel *Vanity Fair*, whilst Stendhal describes it in his *The Charterhouse of Parma*.

The inimitable poet William McGonagall also wrote one entitled 'The Battle of Waterloo', as did both David Buchan and William Whitehead.

Perhaps the shortest was penned by William Wordsworth in February 1816, entitled 'Occasioned by the Battle of Waterloo':

> Intrepid sons of Albion! not by you
> Is life despised; ah no, the spacious earth
> Ne'er saw a race who held, by right of birth,
> So many objects to which love is due:
> Ye slight not life – to God and Nature true;
> But death, becoming death, is dearer far,
> When duty bids you bleed in open war:
> Hence hath your prowess quelled that impious
>   crew.
> Heroes! – for instant sacrifice prepared;
> Yet filled with ardour and on triumph bent
> 'Mid direst shocks of mortal accident –
> To you who fell, and you whom slaughter spared
> To guard the fallen, and consummate the event,
> Your Country rears this sacred Monument!

95 The Lion Mound

THE LION MOUND (or Butte du Lion in French) is a large artificial hill which today towers over the battlefield of Waterloo. Traditionally it is supposed to commemorate the location where Prince William of Orange was wounded by a musket ball in the shoulder during the battle, although it is not in the exact location. It was ordered to be constructed in 1820 by King William I of the Netherlands, but was not commenced until 1824 and completed in 1826.

The monument was designed by the royal architect, Charles Van der Straeten.

Right through the centre of the hillock there is a stone pillar that rises 60ft above the top of the mound and has a total elevation of 201ft. The conical shaped mound was constructed using earth taken from many parts of the battlefield, but particularly from the top of the allied ridge between La Haye Sainte Farm and the sunken lane. The mound is 141ft (43m) in height and

Date of construction:
1826

Location:
Waterloo battlefield, Belgium

has a circumference of 1,706ft (520m), which contains a volume in excess of 13.7 million cubic feet (390,000m³) of soil.

Victor Hugo mentions in his novel *Les Misérables* that on visiting the site two years after the completion of the monument, the Duke of Wellington is said to have remarked, 'They have ruined my field of battle!' but this is almost certainly a myth.

The summit of the hill is reached by 226 steps and the top is surmounted by a statue of a lion mounted upon a stone pedestal. The idea of the lion was suggested by the engineer Jean-Baptiste Vifquain, who conceived it as representing the allied victory – a lion being an emblem of Britain and the House of Orange and a symbol of courage. The lion, which was sculpted by Jean-François Van Geel, has its right front paw upon a sphere, signifying a global victory. The statue weighs 28 tons, has a height of 14ft 6in (4.5m) and a length of 14ft 6in (4.5m). It was cast at the iron foundry in Liège, from where it was brought in pieces by canal barge to Brussels, and then by heavy dray horses to its final site at Waterloo, where it was finally put together.

There is a legend that the lion was cast from brass melted down from cannons abandoned by the French on the battlefield. The statue was, in fact, cast of iron in nine pieces.

In 1832, when the French troops of Marshal Gerard passed Waterloo on their way to support the siege of the citadel of Antwerp, the lion was nearly overthrown by the French soldiers and the tail was broken.

Although seen as an eyesore by some for destroying the shape of the real battlefield, the hill is the ideal place to gain an overview over the entire field of conflict.

96 French prisoner of war gravestone

BETWEEN 4,000 AND 5,000 Frenchmen remained in allied hands after the Battle of Waterloo, not counting the thousands of wounded who lay in hospitals in Brussels. Such a large number of ablebodied prisoners was a headache for the allies as they sought to advance in pursuit of the remnants of the French army and capture Paris. It was therefore decided to transport the prisoners to England as quickly as possible.

They were escorted to Ostend and shipped immediately to Plymouth, where they were landed and had to march over the inhospitable moors to the purpose-built prisoner-of-war camp at Princetown, known as Dartmoor.

The prison was in the process of being emptied of thousands of American prisoners who had been released after peace was finally declared, ending the War of 1812. However, delays in shipping the Americans back home had caused unrest, and in a riot nine Americans had been shot dead and many more wounded. The last American did not leave until 24 July.

Date of construction:
1815

Location:
St Andrew's Church, Ashburton, Devon, UK

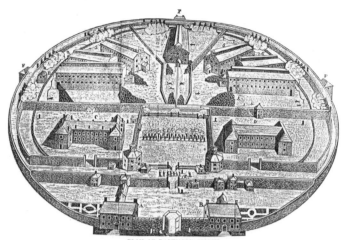

PLAN OF DARTMOOR PRISON
A. The Doctor's House. B. The Governor's House. C. Hospital. D. Petty Officer's Prison. E. Passage between outer wall and railway. F.F.F. Turnkey's Houses. G.G. Public Market and place where the prisoners receive their daily allowances. 1—7. Prisons

Over 4,000 French prisoners arrived at the prison between 1 and 4 July, only two weeks after the battle. Incarcerated in a grey drab prison in the middle of a bleak moor, the prisoners turned their skills to bone carving, leather work and such, utilising the waste from their meals to earn money for additional food or tobacco. Officers were allowed their parole on their honour not to attempt to escape. They could reside at Ashburton, but must not go further than 1 mile from the centre of the town.

The French were kept at Dartmoor until December, when all but those too sick to travel marched to Plymouth to be shipped home. The final French prisoner left Dartmoor in February 1816 and, as they left, the prison gates were locked and the prison closed.

It was not until 1850 that the prison was reopened and it became a penal establishment, as it remains to this day.

Those French prisoners who died were buried there, and the gravestone above records: 'Ici repose François Guidon natif de Cambrai en France, Sous lieutenant au 16th Reg. de Lign, Decede le 18 7bre 1815 age 22 ans' (Here lies François Guidon, native of Cambrai in France, Sub Lieutenant of the 16th Regiment of the Line, died 18 September 1815 aged 22 years).

97 Memorial to the men of the 12th Light Dragoons

who fell at Waterloo

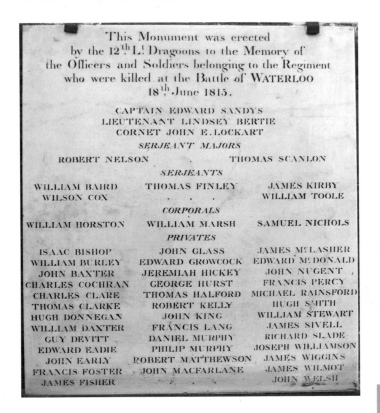

This Monument was erected by the 12th L! Dragoons to the Memory of the Officers and Soldiers belonging to the Regiment who were killed at the Battle of WATERLOO 18th June 1815.

CAPTAIN EDWARD SANDYS
LIEUTENANT LINDSEY BERTIE
CORNET JOHN E. LOCKART

SERJEANT MAJORS

ROBERT NELSON ⋅ THOMAS SCANLON

SERJEANTS

WILLIAM BAIRD   THOMAS FINLEY   JAMES KIRBY
WILSON COX   ⋅ ⋅ ⋅   WILLIAM TOOLE

CORPORALS

WILLIAM HORSTON   WILLIAM MARSH   SAMUEL NICHOLS

PRIVATES

ISAAC BISHOP	JOHN GLASS	JAMES M^cLASHER
WILLIAM BURLEY	EDWARD GROWCOCK	EDWARD M^cDONALD
JOHN BAXTER	JEREMIAH HICKEY	JOHN NUGENT
CHARLES COCHRAN	GEORGE HURST	FRANCIS PERCY
CHARLES CLARE	THOMAS HALFORD	MICHAEL RAINSFORD
THOMAS CLARKE	ROBERT KELLY	HUGH SMITH
HUGH DONNEGAN	JOHN KING	WILLIAM STEWART
WILLIAM DAXTER	FRANCIS LANG	JAMES SIVELL
GUY DEVITT	DANIEL MURPHY	RICHARD SLADE
EDWARD EADIE	PHILIP MURPHY	JOSEPH WILLIAMSON
JOHN EARLY	ROBERT MATTHEWSON	JAMES WIGGINS
FRANCIS FOSTER	JOHN MACFARLANE	JAMES WILMOT
JAMES FISHER	⋅ ⋅ ⋅	JOHN WELSH

FOR CENTURIES, THE deaths of high-born individuals had been commemorated by tablets if not by impressive sculptures or even entire churches. But the deaths of junior officers and private soldiers rarely if ever received any such memorial to mark their passing. Indeed, their anonymous internment in unmarked mass graves, often having been pillaged, stripped and

Date of construction:
1816

Location:
Waterloo Church, Waterloo, Belgium

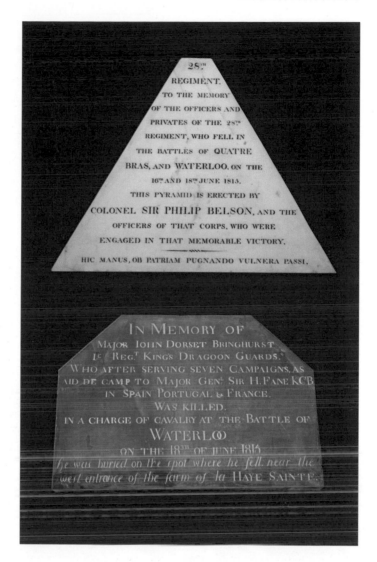

their teeth harshly extracted, did not lend itself to any form of memorial.

But Waterloo formed somewhat of a turning point in attitudes to the remembrance of those who fell in service for their country. With no specific graves to mark, Waterloo Church became the obvious place to erect memorial tablets to remember the fallen.

Memorial stones or sculptures for the nobility still appeared, but more often, the men who fought and died with them were now incorporated into the text.

98 Dutch Silver Cross

THE NETHERLANDS ARMY at Waterloo, with Holland and Belgium then being one kingdom, numbered around 19,000 men, with another 10,000 stationed on the right wing at Hal. Just over half of the Netherlands troops at Waterloo were actually Dutch when the countries split again after the revolution of 1830.

Date of manufacture:
1865

Location:
Private collection

Unlike their allies, the Netherlands troops were not awarded a Waterloo medal, despite their vital services in the early stages of the Battle of Quatre Bras, their maintenance of the farms in the Papelotte sector throughout the Battle of Waterloo and their part in the defeat of one of the three Imperial Guard attacks at the climax of the battle. The majority of these troops fought bravely during the campaign, even though many disparaging remarks were made about them by the British troops.

It was only in 1865, on the fiftieth anniversary of Waterloo, that it was decreed that all Dutch soldiers who had fought in the war of independence (1813–14) or at Waterloo would receive a cross made of silver. It has '1813' imprinted on the obverse and '1815' on the reverse.

Over 30,000 men had served in these wars, but so many had died before the cross was given out that only 5,000 were issued.

The Belgian troops were never granted a Waterloo medal.

Dutch re-enactors.

99 Stratfield Saye House

DURING THE WARS of the seventeenth century British monarchs allowed one-eighth of the value of the conquests made by their armies to be shared by the officers and soldiers who participated. This acted as an incentive whilst not costing the government anything. It was eventually formalised as 'prize money', allocated by prize courts, which adjudicated on matters of eligibility as well as deciding on the value of the prize fund for each campaign or action. A value was allowed for cannon, moneys and supplies captured, and even for cities taken by storm, and a figure to be shared out was derived from this.

Prize money was shared out by rank, each rank of the service being allocated a set number of shares. Once the full number of shares was calculated, the eighth

Date of construction:
1630

Location:
Reading, UK

allocated to the prize fund was divided by the number of shares to work out a value for each share. These payments were then made to the army, often many years after the action had occurred.

The opportunities to earn great sums in land campaigns were rare, but Waterloo was one such example. Payments made for the Waterloo campaign were announced on 21 June 1817 and paid between 25 August and 24 September that year only – any unclaimed sums were then given to Chelsea Hospital. Those in the services would receive it through their pay, all others had to claim personally in London or through their bank from the provinces during this period only.

The Duke of Wellington's shares netted him £61,000 (£2.8 million in modern terms), a captain of a company received £90 7s 3¾d (£4,000), a sergeant £19 4s 4d (£1,000) and a private £2 11s 4d (£150). Unusually, this prize money was also offered to soldiers of all the nations of Wellington's army that fought at Quatre Bras or Waterloo at the same value. Wellington actually gave £40,000 (£1.8 million) of his prize fund to the Treasury.

However, the British government wished to reward the Duke of Wellington for his services to the nation, especially at Waterloo, with an estate, as had been done previously for the Duke of Marlborough, who had received Blenheim Palace. Wellington was given £500,000 for the Peninsular War and £200,000 for Waterloo (around £32 million) to build such an estate. Stratfield Saye, purchased in 1817, was chosen because of its closeness to London and Windsor, and has been the country home of the dukes of Wellington ever since.

Initial plans to destroy the property, originally built in 1630 by Sir William Pitt, and to replace it with a Waterloo Palace to rival Blenheim were eventually shelved. By 1821 wings were added and a conservatory attached. Wellington is often accused of being rabidly conservative and of stifling progress, but it would appear that this was not the case in his domestic life – he had an early form of central heating installed and flushing toilets adjacent to each bedroom in soundproofed rooms.

100 Photograph of Waterloo veterans

LAST SURVIVORS OF WATERLOO IN CHELSEA HOSPITAL, JUNE 1880

John McKay, 42nd Regiment
Aged 95
Wounded at Badajos. Wounded at Waterloo.

Robert Norton, 34th Regiment
Aged 90
Served in Germany, Holland & France

Naish Hanney, 7th Hussars
Aged 88
Served in the Peninsula.
Present at Waterloo.

Benjamin Bumstead, 73rd Regiment
Aged 82
Present at Waterloo,
18th June, 1815

Sampson Webb, 3rd Foot Guards
Aged 82
Present at Waterloo,
18th June, 1815

PHOTOGRAPHY LUCKILY CAPTURED the like-nesses of a number of veterans of the Battle of Waterloo before they all went to their graves. This photograph, taken at Chelsea Hospital on the sixty-fifth anniversary, has an incorrect caption: it is of four Chelsea pen-sioners, all then in their eighties or nineties, who had fought at Waterloo. The fifth, Robert Norton, was not at Waterloo.

The French were also anxious to record images of their veterans and a number of Frenchmen who had served at Waterloo were keen to be photographed in their original uniforms, which they had retained.

The last known British survivor who was actually old enough to fight at the Battle of Waterloo was Maurice Shea of the 73rd Foot who died in 1892; Ferdinand

Date of printing:
1880

Location:
Chelsea Hospital, London, UK

An Old Imperial
Guardsman.

Scharnhorst of the 5th Line Battalion of the King's
German Legion was be the oldest in the British army,
dying in 1893; the last Frenchman, Louis Baillot, died
in 1898.

Officially, the last child present at Waterloo was
Elizabeth Watkins, who survived until 1904. There are
claims that a bugle boy lived until 1905, but the army
did not employ boys as buglers and his claim cannot be
verified.

Monsieur Fabry, 1st
French Hussars.

Acknowledgements

Such a complicated publication requires the help and support of a great number of people and organisations to supply the huge number of high-quality images of the items required. I must therefore heartily thank the following for their inordinate patience and their advice so freely offered regarding the items in their collections. I must particularly thank the staff of the image department at the National Army Museum for the great help I received in obtaining images of the numerous items the museum holds despite the unfortunately timed major refurbishment of the museum now under way. Also to Anne-Catherine Biedermann and Christophe Mauberret, who helped me greatly in navigating the complicated permissions system at the Musée de l'Armée in Paris. To James Scott, deputy curator of the Royal Engineers' Museum for the image of the Waterloo map and Richard Davies, the curator of the Regimental Museum of the Royal Welsh at Brecon for his help in arranging a photograph of the Colours of the 69th Foot to be taken. Andrew Lamb, who kindly allowed me to use the image of Bentinck's serpent from the Bates Collection at Oxford. Olivia Stroud of the V&A Museum, who allowed me to use the images of Wellington's messages written on the battlefield. I must not fail to thank my good friend Mick Crumplin, who unhesitatingly offered images of his personal collection now housed at Wrexham Museum. I must also thank Michael Leventhal and Jo de Vries at The History Press for entrusting such a wonderful project to me; their help and encouragement have been invaluable and greatly appreciated. Finally I must thank my wonderful wife Mary for her forbearance and unhesitating support during what has been both a frenetic and fraught period writing this book.

Gareth Glover

Index

Ainslie, Ensign George 51, 52

Alexander I, Tsar of Russia 217, 267

Amputation 125, 129, 145, 182, 233, 237, 279

Antwerp 168, 199, 262, 264, 278, 301

Artillery 21, 23, 40, 78–9, 85–7, 100–1, 103, 140–1, 145, 149, 151, 164–5, 172, 175, 191, 195, 221, 233, 283,

Baring, Major George 142–3, 151,

Barrington, Ensign the Honourable Samuel 297

Bathurst, Lord 99, 209, 241, 255

Bell, Sir Charles Surgeon 279

Belle Alliance 85, 197, 221, 236

Bellerophon HMS 8, 289–91

Berthier, Marshal Louis 109

Blackman, Captain John 297

Blücher, Marshal Gebhard 13, 37, 39, 40, 44–5, 67–9, 109, 126, 145, 197, 201, 237, 239, 271

Bois, Marie Tete du 262

Boulter, Private Samuel 247

Bowles, Captain George Coldstream Guards 32

Brown, Captain Thomas 297

Brunswick, Frederick Duke of

Brunswick troops 12, 27, 55–7, 102–3, 175, 192

Brussels 26, 31, 33, 39, 44, 45, 56, 61, 72, 74, 75, 77, 91, 99, 103, 113–5, 128–9, 142, 165, 167, 179, 185, 207, 237, 239–40, 262, 264, 267, 278–9, 295, 296, 301, 302,

Bulow, General Freidrich von 197, 202–3, 225

Busgen, Major 81, 147, 188

Bylandt, Major General Willem van 267

Byron, Lord 33, 298–9,

Cambronne, General Pierre 227–8, 283

Chasse, General David 208, 221

Clarke, Volunteer Christopher 52

Clinton, Lt General Sir Henry 103, 208, 289

Clyde, Lt John 297

Colborne, Lt Colonel Sir John 208, 221

Congreve, Sir William 139–41

Cooper, Astley Surgeon 258

Copenhagen, horse 37, 77, 211, 274

Cotton, Troop Sgt Major Edward 9, 244–5, 296, 297

Craan, William Benjamin 266–7

Cromie, Lt Michael 297

Cuirassiers 40, 41, 47–9, 51–2, 91, 93, 134, 151, 161,

Dartmoor Prison 302–3

Delancey, Lt Colonel Sir William 62–3, 261, 297

d'Erlon, Comte 40, 53, 85–6, 88, 89, 91, 95, 114, 131, 141, 143, 161, 203, 233,

d'Honneur, Legion 42–3

Donzelot, General Xavier 52

Dragoons 53, 64, 96, 114, 119, 161, 230, 240

Druout, General Antoine 71

Elba, Isle of 13, 23, 56, 89, 109, 177, 216, 227

Fauveau, Carabinier Francois 47

Forbes, Captain Honourable Hastings 297

Frederick, William King of Prussia 68, 157,

Frischermont 127, 147

Genappe 61, 87, 192, 197–8, 203, 237, 269, 271

General Service Medal 205, 255

George III King 17, 149, 273

Ghent 167–9

Gneisenau, Lt General August von 45, 68, 69, 109

Good, Surgeon Samuel 181

Gordon, Lt Colonel Honourable Alexander 8, 77, 174–5, 297

Gore, Captain Arthur 267

Grose, Captain Edward 297

Grouchy, Marshal Emanuel 39, 44, 126–7, 202–3

Guards, 1st Foot 207, 209, 297

Guards, 3rd Foot 82, 174

Guards, Coldstream 32, 81, 83, 113, 136, 188, 297

Halkett, Colonel Hugh 208, 227

Hanoverian troops 141, 149, 151, 216, 295

Hardy, Thomas 299

Hay, Ensign James Lord 297

Haye Sainte La 53, 62, 85, 91, 93, 99, 142–3, 147, 151, 175, 178, 185, 211, 216, 283, 285, 300

Helena, St 14, 25, 155, 291

Hill, General Lord 229, 285,

Hornn, Coachman Jean 269–70

Hougoumont 72, 79, 81, 83, 103, 107,

111, 136–7, 147, 151, 173, 181, 187, 207, 245, 262, 283, 297

Howitzer 87, 172–3,

Hugo, Victor 134, 136, 281–3, 301,

Hume, Inspector of Hospitals John 77, 175, 234

Keith, Admiral Lord 291

Keith, Ensign Henry 52

Keller, Major Eugen von 270–1

Kennedy, Clark Captain Alexander 96

Lancers 40, 57, 93, 99, 130–1, 161, 176–7,

Landwehr, Prussian 156–7

Larrey, Surgeon Dominique 144–5

Le Caillou 70, 221, 250–1, 269

Lennox, Lt Lord George 114

Life Guards 91, 93, 133, 223

Ligny, Battle of 39, 40, 44–5, 69, 107, 157, 220, 277,

Lloyd, Major William 297

Lobau, Georges Mouton Comte 86, 197, 202–3, 225,

Louis XVIII, King of France 23, 37, 109, 167–9, 171, 228

Mackworth, Captain Digby 229

Maclaine, Major Archibald 297

Maitland, Major General Peregrine 114–5

Maitland, Captain 8, 289–91

Marbot, Colonel Jean Baptiste 8, 126–7,

March, Captain the Earl of 216

McMullen, Private Peter 262–3

Mercer, 2nd Captain Alexander 103, 191–3,

Middle Guard 208–9, 221, 224

Miller, Captain William 207

Milnes, Lt Colonel William 297

Mont St Jean 73, 91, 128, 181, 216, 262

Mudie, James 289

Napoleon Emperor 7, 8, 9, 11, 13, 14, 19, 21, 23–5, 31–2, 35, 36, 39, 40, 42, 43, 44–5, 47, 49, 56, 68–9, 71–2, 74, 89, 95, 101, 103, 109, 120, 126, 127, 144, 146, 150, 153–5, 161, 162, 167, 168, 177, 192, 195, 197, 198, 199, 202, 203, 207, 216, 219, 221, 225, 227, 236, 251, 265, 269, 270–1, 281, 282, 283, 289–91

Nassau troops 12, 81–3, 118, 119, 143, 146–7, 188

Ney, Marshal Michel 39, 40, 44, 45, 52, 76, 147, 177

Northumberland, HMS 291

Nostitz, Major von 45

Old Guard 198, 209, 219–20, 224, 225, 228

Oldfield, Captain John 61–3

Ompteda, Baron 151, 216,

Orange, William Prince of 62, 114, 215–6, 267, 300

Ostend 167, 240, 302

Papelotte 72, 85, 119, 147, 307

Percy, Major the Honourable Henry 239–41

Peruvian, HMS 240

Pistrucci Medal 254

Philips, Captain Frederick 223

Picton, Lt Gen. Sir Thomas 88–9, 103, 130

Pitt-Lennox, Cornet Lord William 114

Plancenoit 72, 73, 107, 157, 197, 198, 202–3, 220–1, 225, 236

Prize Money 19, 271, 308–9

Prussian troops 12, 13, 14, 25, 35, 39, 43–5, 55, 65, 67–9, 71, 72, 87, 105, 109, 111, 119, 126–7, 145, 147, 156–7, 161, 193, 197–200, 202–3, 215, 216, 220–1, 225, 237, 239, 240, 269–70, 283, 287, 290, 295

Quatre Bras, Battle of 31, 33, 39–41, 51, 52, 56, 62–63, 76, 89, 103, 130, 147, 177, 191, 207, 216, 253, 262, 269, 271, 277, 296, 307, 309

Regent, Prince 55, 77, 118, 119, 209, 212, 239, 241, 253, 254

Reille, General Honore 86

Richmond, Duchess of 27, 31–3, 56, 89, 216, 240

Richmond, Duke of 32–3, 113–5

Scots Greys 86, 95, 96, 131, 177, 239, 247, 263

Scott, Sir Walter 62, 135, 213, 295, 298

Shakespear, Captain Arthur 222

Shaw, Corporal John 133–5

Shrapnel 78–9, 140, 173

Siborne, Lt William 285–7

Smith, Volunteer Charles 263

Smith, Private Robert 230

Smyth, Lt Colonel James Carmichael 61–3

Soult, Marshal Jean de Dieu 71, 109, 127, 203

Southey, Robert 298

Spearman, Lt Charles 297

St Helena 14, 25, 155, 291

Stables, Lt Colonel Edward 297

Stiles, Corporal Francis 96–9

Stothert, Captain William 297

Stratfield Saye 37, 308–9

Thackeray, William 33, 299

Tussaud, Madame 244, 271

Uhlans 57, 64, 126,

Uxbridge, Henry Paget Earl of 93, 110, 111, 233–5

Victoria, Queen 212, 255, 296

Vienna, Congress of 7, 13

Waters, Lt Colonel John 62, 63

Wellington, Arthur Duke of 7, 8, 13, 14, 17, 21, 31, 32, 33, 35–7, 39, 40, 45, 56, 61, 62, 67, 69, 71, 72, 74, 75, 76, 77, 83, 85, 86, 87, 88, 89, 91, 95, 99, 100, 101, 102, 103, 107, 109, 110, 114, 123, 131, 140, 142, 143, 145, 147, 168, 169, 174, 175, 191, 195, 197, 198, 199, 203, 209, 211, 212, 213, 215, 216, 221, 233, 234, 237, 239, 249, 261, 267, 273, 274, 283, 287, 301, 309, 313

White, Captain RN 240

Wilberforce, William MP 295

Wordsworth, William 299

Worsley, 1st Lt Thomas 204–5

Young Guard 197–8, 203, 220, 224–5

Also available from The History Press

WATERLOO
1815

THE BRITISH ARMY'S DAY OF DESTINY

GREGORY FREMONT-BARNES

9780752462110

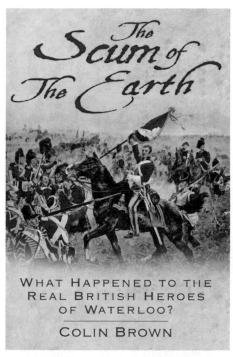

The Scum of The Earth

WHAT HAPPENED TO THE REAL BRITISH HEROES OF WATERLOO?

COLIN BROWN

9780750961851

BRITISH NAPOLEONIC UNIFORMS

THE FIRST COMPLETE ILLUSTRATED GUIDE TO UNIFORMS, FACINGS AND LACE

C.E. FRANKLIN

9781862274846

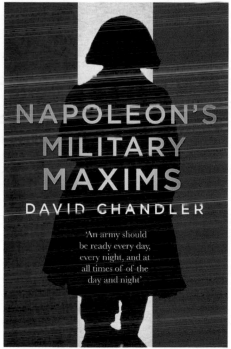

NAPOLEON'S MILITARY MAXIMS

DAVID CHANDLER

'An army should be ready every day, every night, and at all times of of the day and night'

9780750964241

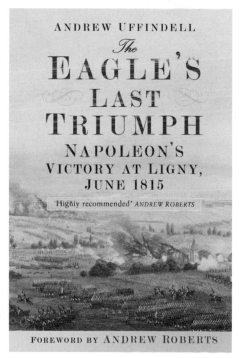

ANDREW UFFINDELL

The EAGLE'S LAST TRIUMPH

NAPOLEON'S VICTORY AT LIGNY, JUNE 1815

'Highly recommended' *ANDREW ROBERTS*

FOREWORD BY ANDREW ROBERTS

9780750956857

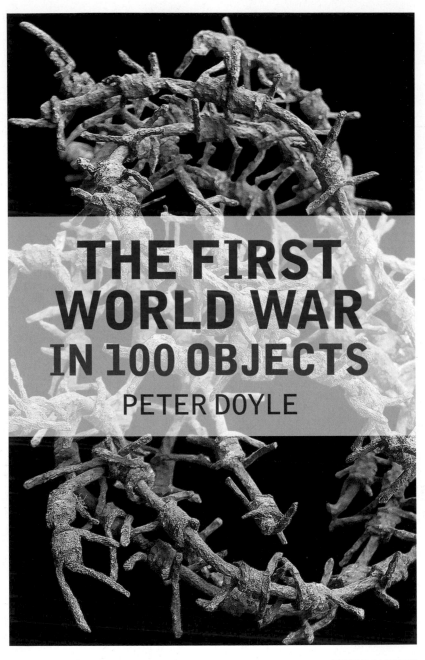

THE FIRST WORLD WAR IN 100 OBJECTS

PETER DOYLE

9780752488110